Computers in the Professional Practice of Design

Computers
in the Professional
Practice of Design

Karen M. Brown & Curtis B. Charles

McGraw-Hill, Inc.

New York San Francisco Washington, D.C. Auckland Bogota
Caracas Lisbon London Madrid Mexico City Milan
Montreal New Dehli San Juan Singapore
Sydney Tokyo Toronto

Library of Congress Cataloging-in-Publication Data

Brown, Karen M.
    Computers in the professional practice of design / Karen M. Brown ,
    Curtis B. Charles.
        p.   cm.
    Includes index.
    ISBN 0-07-011075-1
    1. Architectural design --Data processing. 2. Architectural
drawing--Data processing. 3. Computer-aided design.   I. Charles,
    Curtis B. II. Title
    NA2728.B76   1995
    720 ' .28 ' 5--dc20   94-25997
                                                                          CIP

1 2 3 4 5 6 7 8 9 0   DOC/DOC   9 0 9 8 7 6 5 4

ISBN 0-07-011075-1

The sponsoring editor for this book was Joel Stein.

Printed and bound by R. R. Donnelley & Sons Company.

This book is printed on acid-free paper.

v

Contents

PREFACE

Even though no one knows what the future holds, trends tell us that the nineties and beyond will see more and more small businesses. The economy is forcing us to rethink the way we do business. In order to maintain their profit margins, big businesses are paring down to their core competencies, downsizing their workforce, and contracting out many services that once were performed in house.

This trend, coupled with affordable computer technology, is fueling the increase in the number of new business startups. Resources formerly available only to big businesses are now in the hands of the masses. Many professionals, some laid off from larger firms, will be making use of the technical training they received from their former employers and going into business on their own.

Success in this new marketplace will depend on two things -
1) Willingness to embrace the technology and,
2) Ability to communicate with and respond to
client's needs.

Computer technology will increase productivity by increasing the number of tasks we are able to accomplish during a given time period. It will allow us to maintain a professional image even though our office is located in the spare bedroom of our townhouse. Technology frees us from the repetitive tasks involved with running a business so that we can provide first class service to our clients. The benefits make it imperative that we incorporate computer technology into our offices today.

Small businesses, by nature of their size and structure, are able to respond quickly to market forces and take advantage of opportunities sometimes missed by larger firms. There is less bureaucracy to deal with in the decision making process in the smaller firm. On the other hand, small business is more vulnerable to disaster because it is more sensitive to events like the loss of a client, since the loss of a single client can impose a serious financial burden.

With that in mind, this book was written to enable small to medium - sized businesses to make the most of their strengths through incorporating computer technology into their office.

Use your computer, together with electronic information services to access the latest information in your area of interest and to give yourself a jump on your noncomputerized competition. Use it to give your clients your very best by offering services based on cutting - edge technology, by maintaining a high level of quality control over the services you offer, and by being available to cater to your clients needs. When you computerize your office, you will be able to realize those benefits and more.

Some of the software packages alluded to in this book are fairly simple, while others require more effort and practice from the user. We have attempted to provide a variety of answers to the question "How do I integrate computers into my design practice?" so that you can make an informed decision. The solution you choose will be up to you.

There will be many issues to address and many challenges to meet. Those of us who are best able to meet these challenges will be successful in the future.

ACKNOWLEDGMENT

The layout and design for this book was created electronically by its authors, Karen M. Brown and Curtis B. Charles, principals of C4 STUDIO using Microsoft Word, Claris Works, and Aldus PageMaker on Apple Computer's Mac IIci, equipped with Radius 33 MHz – 68040 Rocket and Daystar Digital Turbo 040 – 33 MHz accelerator boards. Additional hardware included Iomega 150 Multidisk, Microtek ScanMaker IIxe flat bed scanner, Radius Display/21 color monitor, NEC Intersect CD-ROM, Calcomp Drawing Board II with Calcomp's pressure sensitive pen, Radius VideoVision video capture card, and Radius Precision color display 24 bit interface card.

Art was produced using Aldus Freehand, Aldus Gallery Effects, Adobe Illustrator, Adobe Photoshop, Adobe Dimensions, Strata Type 3D, Pixar Typestry, Autodessys Form Z, and StrataVision Studio Pro,

Page proofs were printed on Calcomp CCL 600 laser printer, Calcomp ColorMaster Plus thermal wax printer, RasterOps 300i dye-sublimation, and final camera ready book typeset on LaserMaster Unity 1200 dpi printer.

We would like to take this opportunity to express our thanks to all the public relations, product managers, and technical support staff of all the software and hardware companies that took the time to participate in the realization of this book.

In addition, we would like to thank our sponsoring editor Joel Stein, for giving us the opportunity to write this book.

Finally, we would both like to thank Howard University and Massachusetts Institute of Technology for giving us the academic foundation to add our literary contribution to the efficient use of computers in the professional practice of architecture and the design.

For us, this has been a culmination of professional experience acquired at HMV Architects, Trinidad; Oliver T. Carr, Washington, DC; RTKL Associates, Washington, DC; Kaiser Permanente, Washington, DC; LaForet Engineering, Japan; Howard University School of Architecture, Washington, DC; and, the University of Miami School of Architecture, Coral Gables, Florida.

Thank you all for making this project a success.

Curtis B. Charles, MIT'89

C4 STUDIO©, Modeled with Form•Z, rendered with StudioPro

INTRODUCTION

ince the inception of computer-aided design and drafting (CADD), computers appear to have played a vital role in the practice of architecture, engineering, and their allied professions. This however, is merely an illusion. In fact, because most designers in practice were not formally trained to use computers as a productivity tool, they are unfamiliar with its capabilities. They have not taken advantage of the opportunity to fully integrate this technology into their office in a manner consistent with the practice of architecture and engineering.

The resulting move away from the team concept (pre-computers) to a fragmented system manifested itself in separate groups of designers, draftspersons, project architects and project managers. This practice utilizes designers who develop conceptual sketches for a project. These sketches are then passed on to draftspersons who create design development and construction document drawings for the project architects to use to produce specifications. The project manager then takes the construction documents and specifications through the bidding, permit, and construction administration phases of the project. Although this fragmented system has and still is working for many architectural and engineering firms, it is quite inefficient and can be greatly improved using computers in conjunction with CADD.

Computer technology was intended to make the practice of design more efficient and integrated. However, long after the introduction of computers and CADD, very little can be seen in the form of efficiency and savings in many design firms. The reason for this slow growth is that most design firms are still functioning in the mind set and culture of a fragmented practice. Although firms have bought computer systems and CAD software applications, designers are still sketching on tracing paper and passing their hand-drawn sketches to CADD operators, who then have to convert these sketches into computer-generated drawings.

Even with the prevelation of computers in architectural firms, designers are still using traditional techniques, then passing sketches to CADD operators, instead of beginning the design process on the computer.

Instead, designers can use the computer at the outset to begin the thought process in sketch or 3D form. Design firms operating in an nonintegrated manner will not begin to realize true benefits until there is a complete change in the "thinking process" about technology and its place in the design office. The technology should be used as a unifying force to produce the most efficient and integrated computer design environment.

Studies have shown that approximately 30 percent of the practice of engineering or architecture entails CADD. The remaining 70 percent of each practice is spent on office productivity tasks such as accounting, marketing/project proposals, business development, word processing, contracts, project scheduling, project management, financial feasibility analysis, construction cost estimating, life - cycle costing, fee proposals, operating expenses, payroll, correspondence, meeting planning, transmittals, and building program analysis. Interestingly enough, many design firms have not taken the steps to automate and integrate these office productivity tasks.

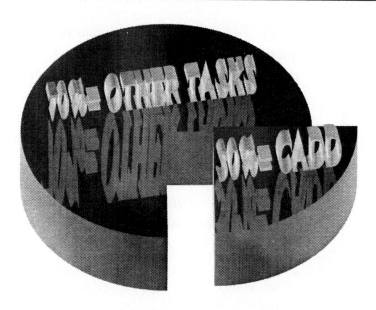

As designers, it is important to remember that CADD accounts for only 30% of the tasks performed in a design office. The remaining 70% relates to bringing work into the office and maintaining a productive practice.

Firms can take advantage of the same computer hardware that occupies only 30 percent of their design firm's day-to-day activities to assist in accomplishing the other 70 percent of the office productivity tasks.

The appropriate use of computer technology presents the design profession with challenges as well as opportunities. The challenges of computer technology are twofold: How can design firms maximize the use of software and hardware technology to remain competitive in the global marketplace, and how can design firms avoid the pitfall of having the computer technology overcome their practice?

The opportunity for designers is quite clear. For a computer to be a full, productive tool, integrated into the design practice, its application must be consistent with how information flows through a design firm. Architecture and design firms must use the computers that they have purchased as design and productivity tools to fully automate and integrate every aspect of their design practice.

"But how ?" you ask.
Well , we invite you to read on.

C4 STUDIO©, Modeled with Form•Z, rendered with StudioPro

CHOOSING THE RIGHT SYSTEM

aving a computer system in a design practice has almost become a necessity, because many clients are now demanding that some or all of a design project be done digitally. As a matter of fact, some government agencies require all projects be submitted in a digital format. This means that everyone on the design team must now be able to communicate design ideas via digital media. This mandate from clients has forced architects, designers, and their consultants into the world of computers and design.

The need for effective communication among members of the design team has led some design firms to implement networks and messaging systems in their offices, to transfer design files, and facilitate correspondence. This is the easiest way for everyone on the design team to work efficiently and accurately. These methods of communication allow everyone on the design team to access a common database of design and project-related information through network systems. Within the design firm, an integrated network of computers can be quite beneficial to other members of your staff who perform other office productivity tasks. For example, sales and marketing personnel can have direct access to the same project database as the design team, from which they can prepare advertising and sales materials.

In order to maintain maximum productivity throughout your design practice, the computer system you choose to incorporate into your practice must be used for more functions than just CADD. Therefore, it is important that a personal computer system be at least a DOS/Windows-based 486 33-MHz IBM compatible or Apple Macintosh II system with a floating-point math coprocessor. Such a configuration ensures that your computers can perform CADD, 3D modeling, rendering, and animations, as well as other vital office productivity tasks.

One of the most important considerations for designers who are thinking of incorporating or expanding their computer capabilities is the ability to purchase a system that can facilitate productivity right out of the box – a system that is easy to learn and very user friendly. If this is a criterion that your firm believes is important when considering an upgrade or purchase of a computer system, then Apple's line of Macintosh and Quadra computers would be the ideal design and office productivity tools for your practice. Since Apple introduced its line of Macintosh computers, designers have used these machines as visualization tools to communicate their design ideas. Further, because of its user-friendly graphical user interface and thousands of available software applications, these computers have become indispensable business tools to perform productivity tasks such as financial feasibility analysis, fee proposals, operating expenses, payroll, correspondence, and meeting planning.

With the advent of Apple's high-end computers, and the increased availability of traditional as well as new, powerful and sophisticated computer-aided design applications, the Mac is the ideal platform for designers to create and present 3D models, renderings, environmental graphics, and animations. Almost all the software applications for this platform are consistent with Apple's graphical user interface so that once the designer gets a good understanding of the user interface of one software application, the basis for using other applications would have been learned–saving time and money.

With easy to use and powerful computers like Apple's PowerMacs, you and your staff can spend more time doing what you do best—creating good, functional designs.

If computers are to play a vital role in the practice of design, complementing (not replacing) traditional tools and methods, then the system you choose must be productive right out of the box. This book covers many ways in which the computer and appropriate software applications can increase your productivity when incorporated with the fundamentals of traditional tools and methods.

SELECTING THE RIGHT COMPUTER SYSTEM
OPTIONS:

      IBM OR COMPATIBLE

      MACINTOSH

      WORKSTATION

Which option you choose depends on two major factors:

Needs - What do you want the system to do ?

Cost - How much do you have to spend ?

It is very important to do a needs analysis to help you determine which tool to use.

You don't use a wrench to pound a nail, you use a hammer.

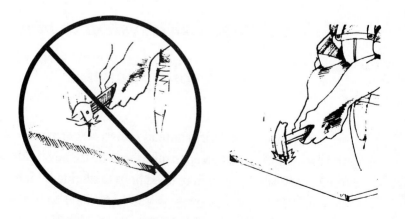

Evaluate your need then purchase the correct tool for the job.

<u>Things to consider in your needs analysis</u>:

1. What tasks do I perform that can benefit from automation?
2. What software is available to facilitate this automation?
3. What hardware platform does it run on?
4. What input and output needs do I have?
   (Scanning, printing, copying, faxing ...)

The other big question is how much you have to spend. With the variety of equipment available, you should be able to put together a system to match your budget.

Whether your firm already uses a computer or is about to purchase a system, you need to take the time to reevaluate all your office productivity needs. You may need help to decide which system to buy. You can ask your colleagues or you may need to hire a consultant to determine what supporting software applications and third-party peripherals need to be purchased to efficiently execute your daily office productivity tasks in an integrated manner.

For 2D and 3D design work, you will need a system with a floating point unit or math coprocessor built in. This is because the software applications you will be using require a lot of "number crunching" to do things like render images and make complex CAD calculations. Be sure not to get trapped with lower-priced systems that do not have these coprocessors.

If you are choosing a second system for your other nondesign office productivity tasks, there are many less expensive options. The base equipment will depend mainly on your software specs, but the possibilities are many. For example, many of the office productivity software applications presented in this book will run on a slightly slower (less expensive) machine without decreasing your productivity.

The next really important aspect of the system is the monitor. After all, this is design and it is very visual.

Radius Precision Color Monitor

MONITORS are available in screen sizes from 12 to 21 inches, measured diagonally. You will need a color monitor for almost all design applications. Look at the specs on a monitor very carefully. There are so many terms to learn and considerations to make that if you are not careful, you could be very disappointed. Expect to pay more for the right monitor. It will save a lot of frustration and will be money well spent.

Here are a few important things to ask about:

Dot pitch - 0.28 or lower. The number represents the distance between individual screen pixels. The smaller the distance, the sharper the picture. This is especially important for rendering applications.

Monitor - 17-inch screens and larger are better suited to graphics and design work. You can display 1 (8 1/2 x 11 in) to 2 (11 x 17 in) pages (as the monitor size increases) without having to scroll.

Monitors that use flat-square or Trinitron tubes typically provide better image quality than the conventional curved tubes.

Screen geometry - Circles should appear round, not oval; squares should have straight, even sides. The focus should be sharp and clear and the colors uniform.

Refresh rate - 70 Hz or higher at all resolutions.

Noninterlaced - Less flicker (vs interlaced)

Resolution - Expressed in dots per inch (dpi), the higher the dpi, the better the resolution, the clearer the picture. 1024 x 768 for graphics and renderings, less (800 x 600 or 640 x 480) for nongraphic applications.

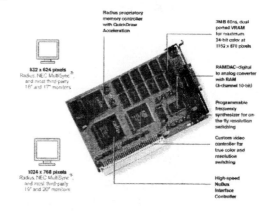

Radius LeMansGT video card. On Apple's Macintosh and PowerMac computers, video cards like this fits into a NuBus slot. On Intel based computers, video cards are installed into an expansion slot once the casing of the computer (CPU) is removed

VIDEO CARD - 8-,16-, or 24-bit video card. Eight- bit allows you to see 256 colors; 16-bit allows you to see 65,536 colors, near photo quality. Twenty-four bit allows you to see 16 million colors, true photo quality.

Depending on the application, you may be able to get by on less than full color (24-bit), for 2D CAD and word processing, but for rendering and other graphic applications, you need a monitor and a video card (inside the computer) that can display true 24-bit color.

Another aspect for your consideration is the memory. The amount of memory on the card affects the quality of the display and the speed at which the card processes information. Video RAM (VRAM) is faster than dynamic RAM (DRAM). A quick chart shows how much RAM will support how many colors at 1024 x 768 resolution.

Memory(in meg)	Color support
1	256
2	65,536
3-4	16 million

Controls - It is important to ensure that the image can be adjusted for contrast, brightness, vertical and horizontal size, and centering of the image on the screen. The better monitors offer even more extensive controls.

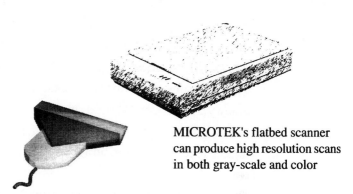

MICROTEK's flatbed scanner can produce high resolution scans in both gray-scale and color

Hand-held scanners like LOGITECH's ScanMan are perfect for small offices.

SCANNERS - A scanner is a device which converts an image to digital information so that it can be understood by your computer. This digitized image can then be used to create your presentation documents after editing with image-editing software or brought into your word processor with the help of OCR (optical character recognition), which actually reads text. Scanners can be gray scale only (black and white) or color. The prices have dropped considerably since scanners were first introduced and a color scanner has become an affordable peripheral.

Depending on the final disposition of the scanned image, you can determine which scanner to purchase. Scanners are classified by the highest resolution at which they scan, for example, 300 dpi, 400 dpi (dots per inch).

For output to your 300-dpi laser printer, without enlargement of the image, there is no need to purchase a scanner with a scanning resolution higher than 300 dpi. If, however, you plan to enlarge or output images at a higher resolution, say typeset quality, then you should purchase the higher-resolution scanner. For extensive text scanning, resolutions of 400 dpi or higher lead to more accurate scans.

If you only scan the occasional, small-sized image and office space and price are primary considerations, then a hand-held scanner could be for you. If you are a more avid scanner, you will need a flatbed scanner.

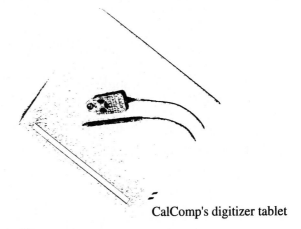

CalComp's digitizer tablet

OF MICE AND PENS

For the purpose of drawing, a digitizer tablet with a puck or pen is the device of choice. It is a high-resolution device which is ideal for the detailed graphics and CAD work that is done in the traditional design office.

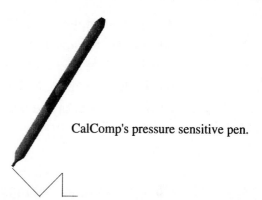

CalComp's pressure sensitive pen.

For those whose computing strokes will have a more artistic flair, the stylus (a penlike device) can be used in conjunction with the digitizer tablet. The stylus gives more freedom of motion and you can more closely imitate the strokes you would make with pen on paper. You will have a computer "pen" on digital "paper." Like most other computing devices, the prices have decreased significantly since their introduction, making the digitizer tablet more affordable and available to every design office.

Another penlike option is the pen-mouse. (Appoint)

As its name implies, it is a mouse that you hold like a pen. The advantages are the more familiar feel and the ergonomic benefits (more later on ergonomics); the disadvantage is that the resolution is not as high as with the tablet option mentioned before and so it may be more difficult to get the same degree of accuracy.

If you just need to point and click, maybe on a second computer, the regular mouse is the inexpensive option. If you have limited desk space, then you can use a trackball. You achieve motion by moving the ball with your fingers instead of moving the mouse all over the desk.

Yet another option available for those of us who use our computers, maybe a portable, to give a presentation, is the portable trackball. It is a small finger operated device that fits completely in the palm of your hand. Its size also makes it very convenient for travel.

Fax / Modems
A fax/modem is a device with which you communicate with other computers or fax machines over a telephone line. It is an essential device because it is your link to the world.

Used with communications software, you can communicate with other computers, bulletin boards, and on-line services like CompuServe, Prodigy, and America Online; even the AIA (American Institute of Architects) has an on-line service available.

There is also the option of E-mail (which we'll discuss later) and bill-paying on line. You can network with other professionals in your field, sit in on conferences, do research by accessing on-line databases, communicate with software companies like Autodesk to ask questions or chat about their products. Using the fax application, you can fax items fresh from your desktop or schedule your transmissions at a time when the telephone rates are less expensive. You can receive faxes while working in another program on your computer. You can read a fax and send a reply without ever leaving your computer. There is more about communications and why you need to be doing it in the chapter on networking.

An important term associated with modems is the baud rate, the speed at which data is transferred over the telephone line. For example, 9600 baud = 960 characters per second. The faster the baud rate, the less time it will take to transmit the data and, considering you are paying for the call, you should probably buy the fastest you can afford.

The modem speed and the fax speed are not always the same, so check for both speeds in the specs because you might find that you did not get what you thought you paid for. Also, you will want to check the features of the software that is packaged with the modem. Some are adequate, but you might find yourself needing to purchase a separate application if you use your fax/modem a lot.

Another thing to look for in fax/modems is voice capability. The modem can distinguish between a fax transmission, a modem transmission, and a voice transmission and answer the call appropriately. The voice feature is such that you can assign mailboxes to regular callers and leave personal messages to be heard only by them.

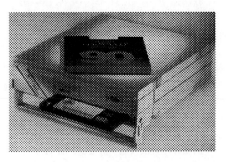

Iomega's storage devices gives one the ability to store data on removable cartridges that currently hold as much as 150 megabytes of information on each. This means that your storage capacity is only limited by the number of cartridges you own.

STORAGE
HARD DRIVES

Taking into consideration the number of applications that you will be using in your office and their storage requirements, you will need at least 200 MB of memory because your hard drive is central to any work you do on your computer. Drawing and painting applications and graphics of any sort are memory intensive. Add to that word processing, project management, and all the other applications discussed in this book, and you will understand why you need 200 MB.

When purchasing a drive, the specs to compare from drive to drive include:

Average access time:

18 milliseconds (ms) or better (do not confuse with average seek time). The smaller the number, the quicker the drive.

Data transfer rate:

1.2 MB per second or faster. The larger the number, the faster the drive.

Compare the cost per megabyte when purchasing your hard drive to give you a basis for comparison. Cost per megabyte = cost of drive / number of megabytes of drive; for example, $300 / 200 MB = $1.50 per MB.

An alternative to fixed hard drives are removable drives. You can purchase the disk drive, then purchase as many disks as you need, building your storage as your business requires. In addition to allowing for expandability, these drives are highly portable and, can be used as backup drives.

NEC CD-ROM READERS

CD-ROM Drives

CD-ROM stands for compact disk - read only memory. It has the ability to store 630 MB of data on a single disk. Like the other technology discussed, prices have plummeted in recent years, allowing many to experience the benefits once reserved for a privileged few. We recommend it as a sound investment (no pun intended).

For the designer, this technology opens up the world of multimedia. Prior to now there was no inexpensive way to store and distribute the enormous amounts of information required by multimedia software applications. Purchasing decisions should, again, be influenced by speed:

> Access times - 250 ms or faster (the lower the number, the faster the drive).

Transfer rates - 150 KB is a single speed drive. The larger the number, the faster the drive.
Buy as fast a drive as you can afford... you will be thankful later.

TAPE DRIVES

Hard disk failures are inevitable. A disk drive's life expectancy tells you the average time before a disk will fail, but it cannot predict when the failure will occur. When failure occurs, if you have not backed up your data, you will lose many hours of work. The moral of the story?

BACKUP, BACKUP, BACKUP!

Tape drives are an insurance policy against hard disk failure and data loss. Between creating new data and changing existing data, you should backup every day. Here as with other drives, speed is a factor but, equally important is accuracy of the restoration and ease of use. If your backup software is tedious, you will probably try to get by without backing up and the consequences will be disastrous. Ask about these features before you purchase.

NOTEBOOKS AND PEN COMPUTING DEVICES

The sizes of computing devices have shrunk over the years to the point where we can carry our computing power with us wherever we go. The nature of the design profession is such that we can benefit tremendously from this improved portability. You can show your clients the solution to their design issues on your portable, right in their office. You can attend meetings and take important notes directly to your computer.

The Personal Digital Assistant (PDA) can send and receive faxes via a fax / modem device.

Imagine having a personal digital assistant (PDA) with you at your next construction site. You can make rough sketches of the site, make design changes or take notes.

This new breed of device can straighten up your lines and produce neat drawings that you can transfer directly to your desktop computer. It can even recognize your handwriting, within limits, to give you a neatly formatted document.

A laser printer like LaserMaster' Unity 1200 is quite flexible because its over-sized printing capacity allows one to output in-house prints for review at 11" x 17" as well as use the printer to out put office documents.

PRINTERS

You have several options from which to choose. First, there is dot matrix, both color and black and white. It is the least expensive option but also the lowest print quality. Still it can be useful in an office situation as a second printer and, it is still the only printer you can use to print duplicates on NCR paper.

Personal lasers are the machine of choice for the small office. You get presentation quality documents at a very reasonable price and there are many options from which to choose. You can purchase printers which will give output at a variety of sizes, too, not just 8 1/2 x 11. You can use the larger size as actual presentation quality or to proof, enabling you to make necessary changes before final output.

Characteristics	Dot Matrix	Personal Laser	Network Laser	Color
Cost	$	$$	$$$	$$ - $$$$
Image Quality	!	!!!	!!!	!! - !!!!
Paper Cost	¢	¢ - ¢¢	¢ - ¢¢	$
Speed	>	>>	>>>>>	>
Ease of use	simple	fairly simple	complex	complex

Network lasers are high-speed printers for use over a network. They feature high-speed processors and buffers to queue print jobs. These printers are meant for use in networked offices with a high volume of printing. Although they are more expensive, it saves having to buy multiple printers and so can be cost effective in those situations.

For color, factors other than the resolution affect the appearance. Is it ink-jet, thermal transfer, or dye sublimation printing technology? The technology differs in quality of output and cost as indicated in the table below.

Characteristics	Ink Jet	Thermal Transfer	Dye Sublimation
Cost	$ - $$	$$ - $$$	$$$ - $$$$
Image Quality	!	!!	!!!

If you primarily need business documentation with a sprinkling of color for effect, like for charts and graphs, an ink-jet printer may be what you need. Thermal transfer printers will give you good color saturation, bright colors, and are fairly easy to use. The disadvantage would be the cost per page. You need to purchase special paper to get consistent and reliable color. Also, thermal printers do not handle continuous-tone images as well as a dye sublimation printer. The dye sublimation printer is the most expensive of the three types of color printers, but it does the best job on continuous-tone images.

The type of printer you choose will be determined by the type of hard-copy output you expect to have in your office situation. The color printer market is still developing and the quality of the output will someday match what we see on the screen. Until then, we still have to resort to service bureaus for really high-end color work.

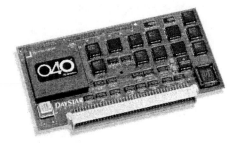 

This Turbo 040 accelerator by DayStar Digital, and the StageTwo Rocket developed by Radius have redefined the term"getting the most out of your investment." Products like these on both Intel-based and Apple computers can be installed in most older computer, giving you today's speed and technology, at a lesser cost than purchasing a new computer.

ACCELERATOR CARDS

The development of accelerator cards has changed the way we make decisions about purchasing computer systems. Design firms that want power and speed but cannot afford to purchase high-end computer systems can purchase an upgradeable midrange computer and an accelerator card for a total price that is less than a high-end system. An accelerator card is a board that you plug into an expansion slot on the motherboard of your computer.

It works by taking over some or all of the processing functions from the motherboard. It is equipped with its own processor and memory. The mechanism by which these boards work differs, but the result is an increase in the processing speed of many functions within the software application.

Some accelerator card manufacturers have introduced the use of multiple cards to simultaneously energize your computer. Radius has developed distributive software that frees the motherboard to process day-to-day productivity tasks, while at the same time, one of their Rocket accelerator cards is being used to process animation sequences, and yet another board is processing another task. These cards are typically used to speed up functions within some of the more popular software applications like Adobe's Photoshop and other CAD and multimedia applications.

A WORD OF CAUTION

Accelerator cards will not speed up all your applications or even all the functions within a particular application and can sometimes interfere with software you are already running. If you are willing to work out the kinks, though, accelerator cards can help you upgrade without purchasing a new system.

C4 STUDIO©, Modeled with Form·Z, rendered with StudioPro

ACQUIRING
THE
CLIENT

or many years marketing has not been an integral part of the practice of architecture, interior design, urban planning, and landscape design. These firms depended heavily on repeat business and referrals. However, as the U.S. economy began to deteriorate in the eighties, we saw many design firms become more aggressive in their marketing efforts. Design firms have learned that in order to meet the needs of demanding clients and a shrinking marketplace, they must become more flexible and *proactive*. They have discovered that in these times of layoffs and cutbacks, an effective marketing strategy that will bring new commissions into the office is of paramount importance to their survival. As a result, marketing has become an indispensable function in the practice of architecture and design, for keeping existing clients and attracting new ones. Marketing is the tool we use to acquire commissions compatible with the firm's practice. However, identifying such specific clients can be quite time consuming using traditional marketing methods. Computers present design firms with challenges as well as opportunities to automate their marketing functions in order to maximize the return on their effort.

Whether you use a marketing staff or charge these duties to principals, computer-aided marketing saves time and money.

All project-related drawings, documents, and presentation materials are easily accessible from the firm's computerized files. Money is saved because, ultimately, an outside marketing firm does not have to be retained. Most of all, in-house computer-aided marketing gives design firms complete control over their marketing plan, allowing them to specifically tailor it to meet the needs of each potential client.

Who is the client?

To identify and market to potential clients in need of your particular services, computers can assist in a variety of ways. Lists to cater to almost everyone's needs are available in computerized form. There are mailing list packages on the market that can provide your firm with useful information about other businesses like location, company profile, demographics, and Standard Industrial Classification (SIC) codes - defining types of business.

ProPhone for Windows - [Select Phone - Southern Region - 2nd Quarter 1994]

File Edit Sort Window Help

Name	Address	City	State	Zip	Telephone	SIC Code
		miam	fl			7011A
VAGABOND MOTEL	7301 BISCA...	MIAMI	FL	33138..	305-757-45...	7011A
ROYAL MOTEL	7411 BISCA...	MIAMI	FL	33138..	305-754-79...	7011A
SEAGLADES MOTEL	1223 NE 1ST...	MIAMI	FL	33030	305-247-66...	7011A
LA QUINTA INN INNS	7401 NW 36...	MIAMI	FL	33166..	305-599-99...	7011A
FALCON MOTOR INN	13330 SW 28...	MIAMI	FL	33030	305-246-52...	7011A
SYLVANIA HOTEL	226 SW 5TH ...	MIAMI	FL	33130..	305-545-71...	7011A
TRADE WINDS MOTEL	4525 SW 8TH..	MIAMI	FL	33134..	305-446-42...	7011A
SOUTH BEACH HOTEL	236 21ST ST	MIAMI.	FL	33139..	305-531-34...	7011A
SOUTH BEACH HOTEL...	236 21ST ST	MIAMI.	FL	33139..	305-531-34...	7011A
CORAL SANDS HOTEL	7800 ABBOTT..	MIAMI.	FL	33141..	305-861-34...	7011A
SHELLY HOTEL	844 COLLINS...	MIAMI.	FL	33139..	305-531-33...	7011A
SKYLARK HOTEL APTS	865 COLLINS...	MIAMI.	FL	33139..	305-538-72...	7011A
TUDOR HOTEL ASSOC...	1111 COLLIN...	MIAMI.	FL	33139..	305-534-29...	7011A
CLIFTON HOTEL THE	1343 COLLIN...	MIAMI.	FL	33139..	305-534-09...	7011A

(c) 1992-1994 Pro CD, Inc. The listings on this product are licensed for your personal use.

Using PROPHONE CD for Business, (a national telephone directory on CD-ROM), you can search for prospects by SIC codes or business headings and retrieve information including address, telephone number, and number of employees.

CD-ROM – massive amounts of information on a compact disk – is a very useful way to acquire and sort all this data in an efficient manner. The prices on these types of drives are no longer prohibitive and we recommend them as a sound investment. Once you define your market, searching through a CD-ROM database can provide you with a good starting point for your marketing effort. Remember, a good list can eliminate a lot of leg work.

Another aspect of the marketing effort comes in determining how you are going to market to these potential clients. Do you use direct mail, telephone calls, newspaper, or television? While your budget will be a big determining factor, having geographic type information on clients may help decide whether direct mail versus newspaper advertising could yield more "bang for the buck." An application that can display your prospects as pushpins on a map may be useful here.

Once the list of potential clients has been finalized, the task of contacting and tracking leads can be handled by contact management applications – customized databases with fields for everything from the name and telephone number to results of contacts and a lot more.

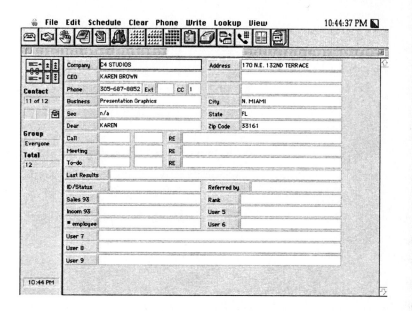

Contact management applications like ACT and FileMaker Pro give you the opportunity to customize data entry according to the way you work. Unlimited notes, activities, and a complete history log are automatically attached to each contact.

These fields can then be sorted individually or in combination, giving design firms the ability to organize information in a manner that makes it easy to disseminate and retrieve marketing and sales materials. Additionally, the report generation feature gives the designer the added dimension of allotting a cost factor of time spent towards marketing. For instance, while conducting "cold calls" or follow-up calls to potential clients, you can:

     * Generate a daily to-do list – calls, meetings

* Take notes during the conversation – to send a brochure maybe.

* Access your calendar to schedule meetings – see conflicts immediately.

* Update client information – may have moved or acquired new computer equipment.

* Time each activity / phone call.

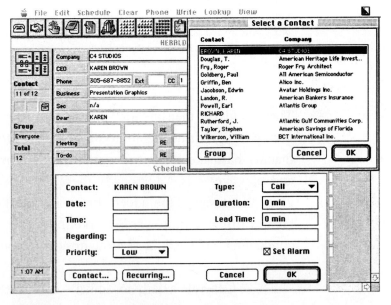

Schedule unlimited calls, meetings, and to-do's without typing, and be reminded even if you're in another software application.

When the telephone conversation is completed, you can:

* Immediately merge the notes from the conversation into a letter template, ready with the client's name and address, confirming the details of your conversation.

* Generate customized reports showing completed and future activities, that is, calls to be made; information to send out; meetings to attend.

* Print your mailing labels directly from database information for your outgoing mail.

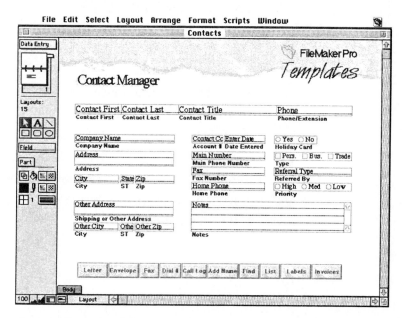

Access client records by name, city, or by other characteristics such as design type or building type.

Compared to a time-consuming manual, Rolodex, and typewriter sequence, the applications illustrated above give a design firm the tools to automate its marketing effort while at the same time, increasing efficiency.

THE SALES PITCH

This marketing effort continues until we find a prospect seeking the services we offer. Once identified, the next step is to get as much information about the client and the project as is available. For instance, project location, budget constraints, expected time of completion, selection criteria for design firms, and other pertinent information to help you prepare an introduction package for this client .

The goal of this introduction package is to get the client's attention and win the commission. To achieve this goal, your package must make the best impression both visually and in content. Design firms need to be innovative and use new ways of presenting design proposals to prospective clients. For this purpose, we want to discuss some applications which, although not traditionally marketed to the architectural and design communities, can enhance your presentations and give you the winning edge.

WINNING EDGE MARKETING COMMUNICATIONS:

Architects and designers, who previously purchased computers solely for CADD, can now utilize their Macintosh or Windows and Windows NT systems in conjunction with desktop publishing and graphic design software to produce effective marketing communications specifically tailored to each potential client, regardless of the size of the design practice.

PAGE LAYOUT PRESENTATIONS

For producing attractive, compelling design proposals and marketing materials, page layout applications are the tool of choice. The page layout applications on the market can help you create both simple and complex layout and designs, handle color and manage publications with sophisticated graphic and typographic capabilities.

Intuitive page layout and production programs give designers the capability to integrate all previously produced sketches, 3D models, renderings, and all project-related graphics with text to create winning design proposals.

Text describing designs can be typed directly in the page layout application or imported from your word processing application where they can be manipulated, mixing and matching font sizes and styles, wrapping text around graphics, and adding color along with many other features to convey the desired image. To ease the task, predesigned templates of brochures, newsletters, financial reports, and proposals have been created. These templates are used as a starting point for the architect and designer to begin developing page layout presentations. Page layout and illustration applications give the designer the ultimate control over printed marketing and sales presentations.

Now, let's go to the gallery to view some examples of how page layout and graphic illustration software applications can be used to create impressive marketing materials.

Where Technology meets Design

ASSOCIATES

3-Dimensional Modeling

Com-pany profile created with Aldus' PageMaker. All the graphics were created with Autodessys's Form•Z and rendered in StrataVision's StudioPro and Electric Image Animation, then imported along with text from Microsoft Word.

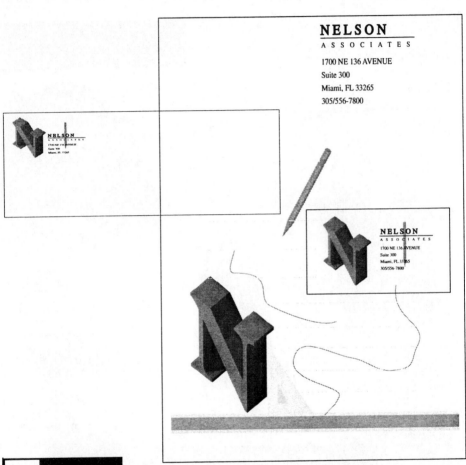

Corporate Identity

This corporate package was
created using Adobe Illustrator,
Adobe Dimensions and
Autodessys form•Z.

This marketing brochure was created with Aldus Freehand.

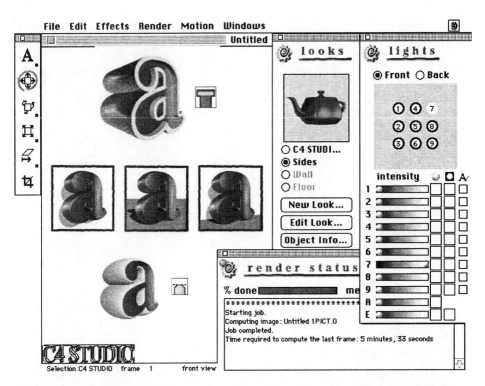

Pixar developed *Typestry* for the creation of three dimensional text design. This software application has tools to apply and adjust textures (materials) and lighting.

Images created using Crystal Flying Fonts Pro and Crystal Flying Fonts ©1994 CrystalGraphics. All rights reserved.

If you only intend to create logo and other text designs, you do not have to purchase an entire rendering package. You can use applications like Pixar – *Typestry* (above), Strata Inc. – *Strata Type*, and Crystal Graphics – *Flying Fonts Pro*. Each of these packages also have the capability of creating simple animation sequences.

An example of the application's advanced capability for designing environmental graphics.

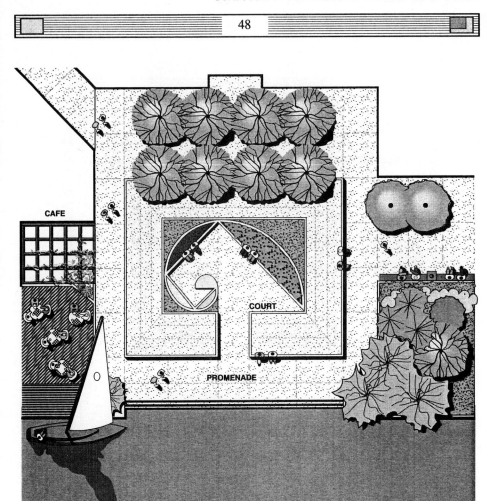

This site plan design shows the versatility and the range of the design tools in Aldus Freehand.

THE INTERVIEW

Another aspect of marketing is the invitation to be interviewed. Once again, the objective here is to impress and convince the client that your firm is capable of receiving his or her commission and has successfully completed similar projects in the past. Your only purpose in this interview is to get the job. Therefore, your firm should do everything within its power to make sure that this objective is achieved. Computers can give you that competitive edge and help target your interview presentation.

DESKTOP MULTIMEDIA PRESENTATION SOLUTIONS

A few years ago it was very cost prohibitive to create presentations on the computer and transfer them to a medium such as videotape. During that period firms were forced to mount their designs on some type of foam-core for presentation purposes.

Slides or overhead transparencies of design work were also used for presentations. Ironically, many design firms still conduct these forms of presentations to potential clients.

However, the cost of producing desktop multimedia presentations has dropped tremendously and is now cost effective enough for design firms to create targeted interview presentations in house. If your firm has been using computers for drafting, you already have the necessary basic computer hardware to be up and running. But what is really propelling this evolution of desktop multimedia presentations is the host of software applications that are being sold with audio, video, graphics, text, animation, and Quicktime capabilities.

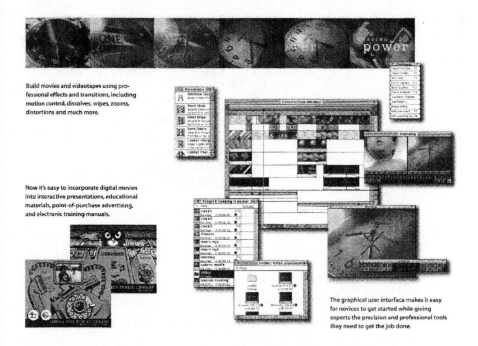

Build movies and videotapes using professional effects and transitions, including motion control, dissolves, wipes, zooms, distortions and much more.

Now it's easy to incorporate digital movies into interactive presentations, educational materials, point-of-purchase advertising, and electronic training manuals.

The graphical user interface makes it easy for novices to get started while giving experts the precision and professional tools they need to get the job done.

Put Your Ideas in Motion.

With Adobe Premier, currently available on Apple's Macintosh, PowerMacintosh, and Intel-based machines your firm can now create high-quality presentations and down-load to video right on your computer. Premier gives you the power and tools to present your firm's image and work to prospective clients with greater impact than ever before.

These applications have made the traditional way of presenting designs on boards, in slide carousels, and on overhead transparencies obsolete. Instead, slide and transparency presentations have moved to the next frontier of the computer desktop where more targeted information can be conveyed to the client–making a more impressive presentation. These software applications' interface will be quite familiar because of their VCR-style remote control buttons that can be used to fast forward, rewind, stop, pause, and play your presentation.

Like page layout applications, these programs are designed to combine sketches, 3D models, and renderings with just enough text to describe the architectural images on each slide or VU-Graph. These applications incorporate an outliner to help the designer organize thoughts in the manner in which the design will be presented. Once the outline has been confirmed and entered into the application, and a predesigned template selected, slide layouts, speaker notes, and audience handouts are automatically generated.

These 35-mm slides were generated from desktop presentation software applications: Microsoft PowerPoint and Aldus Persuasion.

The designer can import elements just as in page layout programs, and each slide or VU-Graph can easily be customized with your company name and logo to create a professional presentation. Some applications include additional software that will allow the designer to link to an overnight slide bureau to quickly produce 35-mm slides. Along with capacity to create 35-mm slides and overhead VU-Graphs, the designer can create an impressive slide show presentation on the computer.

But if you really want to go all out to persuade your potential client, you can add sound, music, special effects, live video on ongoing or past projects, and voice over to your presentation. For such a presentation you will need to add a CD-ROM, speakers, an audio and video capture card, VCR, camcorder, 24-bit video card, and a conversion device to transfer your desktop presentation to video.

Using desktop video systems like VideoVision Studio from Radius Inc., you can now download your stunning presentations from your computer desktop. All you need is a video capture card, your VCR or camcorder, audio speakers, and your existing computer.

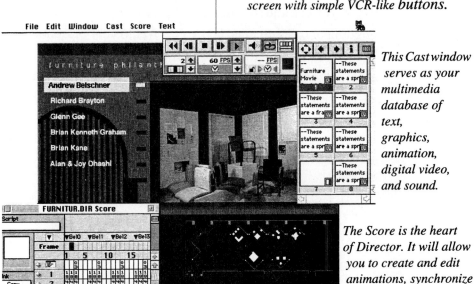

This panel is used to control action on the screen with simple VCR-like buttons.

This Cast window serves as your multimedia database of text, graphics, animation, digital video, and sound.

The Score is the heart of Director. It will allow you to create and edit animations, synchronize media elements, and precisely control transitions, sound, color palette, inks, and tempo.

The interactive design presentation (above) was created using Macromedia's Director (available for Apple's line of computers as well as Intel-based computers). The presentation describes the work of six designers. When the name of each designer is highlighted, examples of their work appear with supporting documentation.

This type of interactive multimedia presentation is one of the most novel and exciting media that designers can use to sell their services to new clients. A good example of this application was the presentation made to the International Olympic Committee by the city of Atlanta in which integrated computer graphics and architecture were used to win the bid to host the 1996 Summer Olympic Games. Interactive multimedia animation involves motion, and thus the designer needs to think like a motion picture director in order to direct a successful presentation.

The objective here is to excite your potential client, and if winning the commission means creating interactive multimedia presentations with music, special effects, and video for the client to experience projects via animated walk-through, fly over, and fly around,

then do it.

You must have a competitive edge!

C4 STUDIO©. Modeled with Form•Z, rendered with StudioPro

PROGRAMMING

rogramming is probably the most important phase in the design process. It molds and gives a solid foundation to the project. Programming is problem-seeking which aims to define goals and give direction to every project. Many clients will provide design firms with a project budget, building footprint, and room sizes. It is the designer's job to do additional investigations, in conjunction with the client, since the data provided is usually insufficient and does not conform to the thinking process of designers, thereby constraining design possibilities.

In pure terms, programming is the collection and organization of facts, the development and testing of program alternatives, the prioritizing of those alternatives to determine real needs, and the analysis of all data collected. Proper analysis of this data will result in a clear statement of the design problem and the development of a design concept where data begins to translate itself into visual design solutions.

HOW CAN COMPUTERS BE USED IN PROGRAMMING?

There are three different types of computer applications that can assist in the task of programming. They are database applications, spreadsheet applications, and mathematical modeling simulations (modeling in this sense is not to be confused with the modeling described in upcoming chapters). We can talk about each of these applications in a little more detail.

DATABASE APPLICATIONS:

Databases are basically software applications which manage and store information of all types. It is the foundation on which many an application is built. Personal information managers and project management applications are just two examples of applications built upon a database foundation. These applications are not your cumbersome, difficult to use, "run of the mill" databases anymore. They have been customized with graphics and user-friendly interfaces to help you navigate your way through the maze of information to find exactly what you need.

Being data-intensive, programming can take advantage of these applications to manage, sort, and present data in a way that is helpful to us.

Many of the computer applications discussed in the project management chapter of this book will provide a lot of useful information from previous designs for use in your upcoming projects.

For example:

        If your firm specializes in hospitals, you can use computers and database applications to easily access your hospital projects ... all the hospitals you have done over the life span of your firm. If you have a 700 - bed project, you can sort this information and say "Let's see all past hospitals over 500 beds." Then, you can get all the project management information for those hospitals – very useful in the programming of another hospital. This will save duplication of a lot of research. For example, instead of having to look up information like the square footage requirements of various hospital work areas, you would have all that valuable information already stored in your project database.

        Now, I can hear you saying " I can already do this! and, you're right, you can. The key questions here are "How long ?!" and "How tedious?!" Believe me, you would much rather search for this information on your computer, retrieving it by entering a few key words, than have to labor through your archives. Think of the dust, think of the frustration, think of the time! Instead, you can simply instruct the computer to prepare a report in which you define the information you want to review and then have it search through the previous projects on file and compile the report.

Also available is database information from CAD packages. Many CAD packages have the ability to interface with databases like Dbase and Oracle to store design information that repeats itself from project to project, such as door and finishes schedules and other design details. Imagine having key elements and details common to many design projects saved in the CAD program of your choice. You can feel confident giving an estimate based on actual costs of past projects. All this, in less than one-fourth the time. This is a productive way to not only access valuable design data but also file and track the data. This is the power of using a computer database.

When firms seek commissions outside of their building type specialty and are designing a project for the first time, computers present designers with the opportunity to build a database of information they can rely on for future projects of the same kind. This is a situation where the program development has to be secured through the traditional methods. However, once all this information is on the computer, it will not only increase productivity for the project at hand, but also for future projects, because now you will be able to return to that information and analyze all the pertinent data.

Spreadsheets

In this context, spreadsheets can be used to display certain mathematical types of data and the relationships between them. Spreadsheet applications such as Lotus 123, Microsoft Excel, or Claris Resolve can be used for tasks such as multiplier calculations, fee proposals, facility programming, building program analysis, life-cycle costing, construction cost estimating, engineering analysis, and financial feasibility analysis. The results of these studies can be displayed in a variety of formats such as bar graphs, pie charts, and line diagrams.

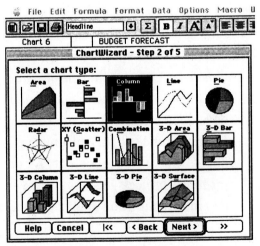

Using applications like Microsoft Excel, Lotus 123, and Claris Resolve, results of studies can be displayed in a variety of formats such as bar graphs, pie charts, and line diagrams in both two and three dimensions.

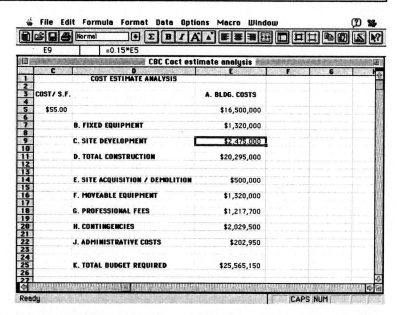

Here, the architect is using Microsoft Excel to calculate professional fees by conducting a "what-if" scenario. Since all the numbers are linked by formulas, changing any fee or cost will result in an automatic recalculation of the other numbers.

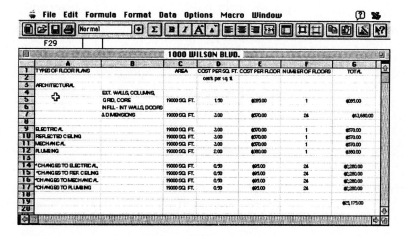

In this example Microsoft Excel is being used to calculate the cost for a CADD job.

MATHEMATICAL MODELING SIMULATIONS

Software applications in this group include Stella and Extend. They use simulations to approximate processes. In the world of design, a project would be defined as the "real system" of which you would build a model. The steps from the start of the project to the end of the project would be represented as "building blocks" in your "system model." Blocks would be linked based on their relationships to each other. As more information becomes available, you can refine and improve your "model" and you can test hypotheses on your "model" before actually undertaking the project.

To illustrate, you can build a computerized mathematical "model" of your hospital project to test circulation patterns on the floor. You will use blocks to represent different areas on the floor. The blocks could contain information on square footage and the number of people who would occupy the area. Then you could simulate various situations, like a full bed count or an emergency, to find out if circulation is adequate or if it needs to be changed. You keep making changes to your model until you have a feasible system.

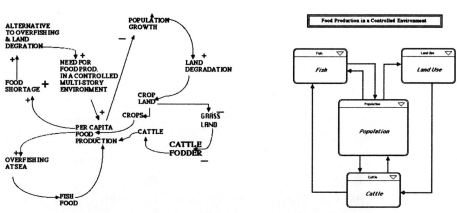

These are examples of system dynamics causal relationship models created by the author for La Foret Engineering in Japan. The models were used in the programming stage of a feasibility design study of food production in a controlled environment. The objective of the models was to analyze the effect of overpopulation on natural resources like land, livestock and fisheries, and then design the appropriate architectural structure to house a hydroponic, aquaculture, hatchery and research facility. This facility could have been built at sea or on land. Using La Foret's Himawari System (piping sunlight via fiber optics), wind energy, hydro energy, and solar energy would make the facility energy efficient as well as environmentally clean.

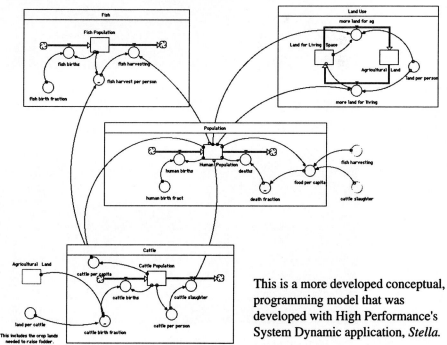

This is a more developed conceptual, programming model that was developed with High Performance's System Dynamic application, *Stella*.

From your system dynamic model you can now proceed to actually building it, confident that you have accounted for every eventuality.

This was one of the resulting designs that presented a solution in which real estate at sea was presented as a viable site to grow food in a controlled environment.

Food production in a controlled environment: on land

While these applications have not been traditionally used in the architecture and design profession, they have been successfully used in branches of operations research and systems dynamics to solve complex problems. As such, the design profession may find it can be instrumental in the programming stage of a project as well.

C4 STUDIO©, Modeled with Form•Z, rendered with StudioPro

CONCEPTUAL
DESIGN

nvariably, a well-prepared program clearly states a design problem and provides a good foundation for the designer to begin conceptualizing ideas and thoughts in direct response to the intended activities of a design project. This is the phase of the design process in which all the data that was collected in the programming phase is now graphically translated and synthesized, beginning to define form, scale, order, space, volume, aesthetics, and character of a project. In other words, the development of a design concept entails the creative bringing together of many elements, that consequently have a direct influence on the design and structure of a project. At this stage of a design project, clear communication is vital and successful concepts must be developed and communicated to the client and design team in a manner that can be understood by all parties.

Whether it is a building, an urban space, an interior or a landscape design, the conceptual design phase of a project begins with ideas that address the problems and objectives such as physical space relationships, circulation flow, human needs, the relationship between the building and its immediate neighborhood, architectural style, site conditions, scale, proportion, and economics. Traditionally, designers have addressed these considerations in 2D plan, elevation, section, and 3D isometrics and perspective, using paper and pencil.

Increasingly, though, the development of computer technology has given designers the ability to produce high-quality conceptual designs for prospective and existing clients and remain competitive.

Some designers may begin the design process by exploring several schematic diagrams such as physical space analysis, relationship analysis, circulation studies, site analysis, scale analysis, functional analysis, aesthetic analysis, technical analysis, building code analysis and zoning code analysis.

Using a digitizer and pressure sensitive pen gives the designer the freedom to begin the design process directly on the computer. Software applications like Aldus Freehand, Adobe Illustrator, Fractal Design Painter and Sketcher, and Alias Sketch are ideal for design development tasks.

All these diagrammatic studies must be put in some kind of architectural or design format that can be understood by designers, consultants, and clients alike.

It is at this point that the designer needs to use a medium to produce documents quickly and accurately. It is important that designers use tools compatible with the fast pace at which concepts and information flow throughout this phase of a design project.

One of the most familiar events in a designer's life is that first lunch meeting when the designer meets a client for the first time and tries to sketch on the back of a restaurant's napkin while the client spills out all sorts of fantastic ideas for a proposed design project.

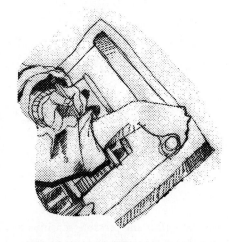

The designer sketches out design ideas.

Some 3D conceptual design applications are as intuitive and simple to use as sketching on the back of a restaurant napkin. Unlike sketching on tracing paper, these design tools give designers the flexibility to work in three dimensions and later generate plan and elevation views.

Instead of beginning the design process by sketching on tracing paper, designers can now use *intuitive conceptual design computer software*. These software design tools give designers the ability to sketch their ideas directly onto the computer as they evolve. 2D illustration design applications use a simplified palette with different drawing tools that allow the user to begin formulating rough, free-form sketches.

2D

3D

Let us take a closer look at the palette of available tools. You can use the pen to draw and the brush for painting. Each document has a ruler available so that your drawings can be drawn approximately, to scale. A freehand tool allows you to sketch as easily as you would with a pen and paper. A nice feature is the autotrace tool. It allows you to use an already existing document, after digitizing it, and have the program trace the outline so you can incorporate it into your design. The 2D sketching programs offer tools to draw circles, squares, and rectangles where you can effortlessly establish the dimensions. In 3D, the tools exist for basic shapes like spheres, cylinders, and cubes to be created just as easily as their 2D counterparts. In addition, you can duplicate, rotate, reflect, scale or apply a shear to any object that you draw.

Finally, you can apply color to your sketches and give your concepts a rather polished look.

With an unlimited number of layers, the designer has the flexibility to organize conceptual sketches by naming and rearranging layers so that specific concepts can be developed on different layers. With "undo" and "redo" functions, the designer can explore and experiment with confidence, creating architectural concepts and testing ideas. The possibilities are limitless.

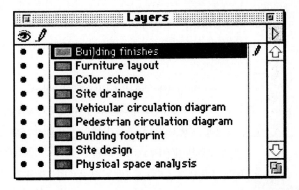

These are some of the layers you might create for design analysis while doing your conceptual sketches in software applications like Adobe Illustrator

These applications are fast and transparent and will automatically update your design as you progress. They are accurate visual thinking tools that can give you instant "on-screen" feedback in two as well as three dimensions, helping to develop your ideas.

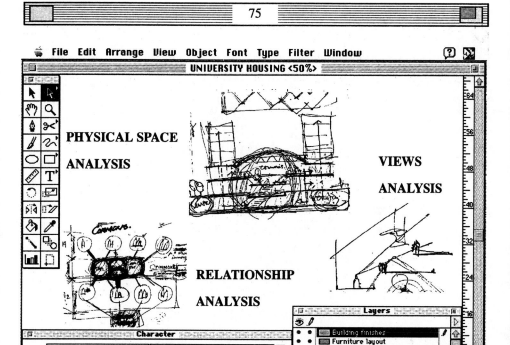

Conceptual design, and design development studies like those illustrated on this page and the next can be created using the advanced graphic communication tools of Adobe Illustrator.

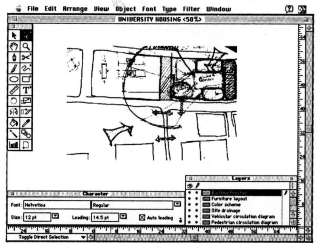

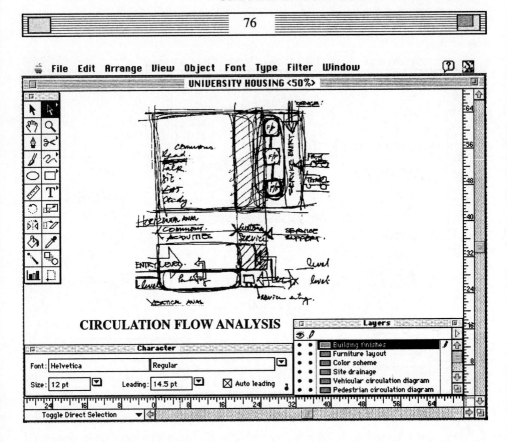

These *intuitive conceptual design computer software* packages give designers the power to effectively express, communicate, and explore alternative design solutions.

C4 STUDIO©, Modeled with Form•Z, rendered with StudioPro

PROJECT
MANAGEMENT

nce a firm acquires a design project, achieving the proper balance of information, budget, and personnel often requires the full-time services of a project manager. Each design project is unique in that it is a one time occurrence whose scope of work can be categorized into definable activities and deliverables. Constrained by a tight budget and definite start and end dates, each activity has to be tracked, scheduled, and managed to ensure efficiency and maximize productivity. It is the project managers' responsibility to anticipate and resolve problems, obstacles, changes, and any resulting delays that occur throughout the project.

Communication is the essence of project management . Accurate and current information about what has happened, what may occur, and necessary changes to the project needs to be constantly communicated to the members of the design team, the client, and all contracted consultants on a regular and timely basis.

Integrating computers with project management and scheduling applications into your firm's office productivity activities can help you direct, schedule, track, and organize all project activities and personnel for the length of the project.

Proper automation of this process enhances communication so that everyone knows the status of each phase of the project; goals are understood; and each individual involved in the design process becomes accountable.

In the planning stage of a design project, your computer can help you define specific activities and work tasks, assign and allocate resources, coordinate these activities, prepare work schedules, and develop an acceptable budget. These tasks can be controlled by:

1) Measuring performance
2) Evaluating options
3) Suggesting corrective action when needed.

Today, the project record book is replaced by project management software applications. All activities, decisions, dates, and conferences related to the project can be entered and more accurately tracked. Once on the computer, principals, partners, associates, project designer, project architect, project manager, job captain, and all consultants will have access to one common project information database for report generation and project consistency. Documents such as change orders, shop drawings, applications for payment, and schedule changes can be issued and accessed by all parties involved.

The benefits of using project management and scheduling software applications in your design practice are as follows:

* They are easy to use and understand. The graphical representation of the steps or tasks involved in the project encourages the user to account for every facet of the project.

* "What-if" scenarios can be presented and analyzed. You can immediately see the effect that adding or shifting resources will have on your project. You can see the impact of changing any of the variables before doing it for real. Potential problems can be anticipated and accomplishment recognized.

* The progress of the project can be tracked against existing design decisions, and members of the design team can immediately react to conflicts.

*Design and redesign costs can be tracked.

*You can have instantaneous access to important information about the project at any time, customized to fit your needs.

*You can create time-scaled diagrams for the project team that show each activity's progress and responsibility and highlight critical pathways and key activities.

Beginning to use these applications will require that you initially input information concerning clients, vendors, consultants, and employees. The beauty of this is that you only have to do it once. When defining the activities for a particular project, the same information can also be used in other projects. For each activity, resources of people and time are assigned. You can also define the end date and work backward. Employee resources can be assigned to more than one project at the same time. For instance, a designer can be assigned 40 percent of the time to Project A and 60 percent of the time to Project B. You can define your calendar to take holidays and weekends into account when calculating dates until a project ends, and calendars can even be customized to reflect an individual employee's unique days and hours. The data can be used for every other project that you are working on, now and in the future. The information is used throughout the project for everything from client billing, to employee time tracking and productivity evaluations, to project evaluation by cost, category, and task.

Some of the high-end products on the market offer even more innovations by keeping track of design-specific and architecturally specific documentation like dunning letters, submittals, and change orders.

Following is a list of some of the features available in the project management applications designed specifically for the architectural profession.

MANAGING CHANGE ORDERS :

It is important to use your project management software to enter all contracts pertaining to a design project. In this way, as contract changes occur and requisitions are submitted, your firm will be able to record and track all approved and pending change orders and their amounts.

MONITORING CONTRACT COSTS :

The cost worksheet serves as a conduit for collecting and analyzing each contract and purchase order for the project. Once this data is entered in the cost worksheet, the application can track all project costs, approved or pending, as well as estimates and revisions. The accounting-like worksheets keep track of budgeted funds versus actual costs. Variances are calculated, warning you of projected overruns.

TRACKING SUBMITTALS:

Shop drawings, specifications, and samples have to be recorded and reviewed during the course of a project. You can track who is responsible for the review of a particular phase, record arrival and departure dates, and determine whether the review period has expired. Additionally, you can flag those running behind schedule and automatically print dunning letters to be sent to them.

RECORDING MEETING MINUTES:

With so many different principals involved on a design project, it is important to keep track of all decisions that affect the project. Since these decisions are often made in meetings, it is vital that the content of these meetings be communicated to each person involved with the project. You can keep the meeting minutes within the project management application, attaching it to the project to show who was in attendance, what items were discussed, what decisions were reached, and who is responsible. These generated minutes can also be sent electronically to each of the team members.

The Project

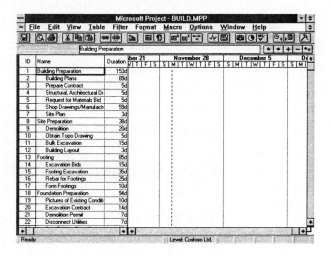

Define the individual tasks.

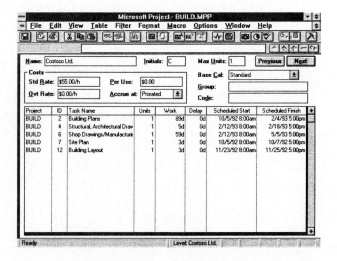

Assign resources to complete the tasks.

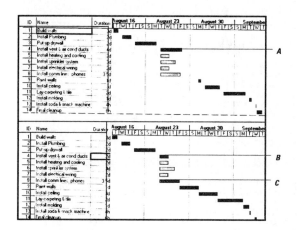

Using project management software like Microsoft Project, MacProjectPro, and Primavera Project Planner, designers can track and manage a project through each phase.

```
Sorted By:To/From/Contract Number   CONTRACTS                        DSGN
Number:CON-91-02921     Spec Sec:        Engineering Services   Date:01NOV91
To    :AZTEC     JS               From:DESIGN    CA
Aztec Engineering Company         The Design Group
101 Main Street                   1215 Ventnor Avenue

Princeton           NJ    19245   Philadelphia          PA    19000
Terms    :<consterm>                              Start Date    :
Manager  :Chris Atkinson                          Completion Date:

THIS CONSULTANT CONTRACT is for the following engineering services:
Value Engineering to be performed at the Design Development Phase.



                                           Net Cost   :$    20000.00
Ref. No.:                        Tax Rate: 0.00% Tax :$        0.00
Accepted:James Strout            Date:06NOV91  Freight :$        0.00
Accepted:Chris Atkinson          Date:08NOV91  Total Cost:$   20000.00

Commands: Add Codes Delete Edit Find Help Issue Print Return Sort View Window
Windows : Address  Costing  Description  Summary
```

Contract

With Primavera's Expedition you can use pull-down menus to enter and track your contracts, and many other project documents.

```
                        Standard Reports                              SCON

  Number Series                                        Copies    Type

  ST-0005      Correspondence Received Today              1      Tabular
  ST-0006      Correspondence Received by Vendor - Last 2 Weeks 1  Tabular
  ST-0007      Transmittals to Vendor by Date             1      Tabular
  ST-0008      Transmittals in Numerical Order            1      Tabular
  ST-0009      Transmittals Sent Today by Vendor          1      Tabular
  ST-0010      Transmittals Sent in Last 2 Weeks          1      Tabular
  ST-0011      Transmittals Sent Within Date Range        1      Tabular
  ST-0012      Transmittals Sent to Specific Vendor       1      Tabular
  ST-0013  W   Unresolved Notes by Ball-in-Court          1      Tabular
  ST-0014      Meeting Minutes Recap by Meeting           1      Tabular
  ST-0015  W   Daily Field Activity for this Week         1      Tabular
  ST-0016      Weekly Materials Delivered by Spec         1      Tabular
  ST-0017      Weekly Field Labor Report, by Vendor       1      Tabular
  ST-0018  W   Weekly Equipment Used by Supplier          1      Tabular
  ST-0019      Visitors at the Jobsite this Week          1      Tabular
  ST-0020      Submittals by Spec Section                 1      Tabular
  ST-0021      Submittals Not Submitted                   1      Tabular
  ST-0022      Submittals Approved                        1      Tabular
  ST-0023  W   Submittals Not Approved                    1      Tabular

  Commands: Add  Find  Help  Return  eXecute
```

To facilitate routine reporting, Primavera's Expedition groups the reports that you would run each week or month. You can then execute all reports in a series at one time.

```
                   APPLICATION AND CERTIFICATE FOR PAYMENT              DSGN
  Contract To  :
          From:
          No. :                                              Appl No:
                                              Certified: N Period To:

  Change Orders Approved in This Period    Original Contract Sum .. $      0.00
                                           Net Change by C.O. ..... $      0.00
   No.   Date   Additions   Deductions     Contract Sum to Date ... $      0.00
                                           Compl & Stored to Date . $      0.00
                                           Percent Complete ....... $      0.00
                                           Retainage:
                                              0.00 of Compl Work  $        0.00
                                              0.00 of Stored Matl $        0.00
                                                 Total Retainage .... $     0.00

                                           Total Earned - Retain .. $      0.00
                                           Tax to Date ............ $      0.00
                                           Total Prev Amount Cert . $      0.00
  Current:$      0.00 $         0.00 Current Payment Due .... $      0.00
                                           Balance to Fin + Retain $      0.00
  Prev  :$      0.00 $         0.00
  Total :$      0.00 $         0.00       Amount Certified..... $      0.00

  Commands: Add  Certify  Del  Edit  Find  Get  Help  More  Print  Return  Window
  Windows : Detail  Summary  Text
```

Application for Payment

```
ALL    By:Type/To/From         CHANGES                          DSGN
Type:AMD  To:DESIGN   CA        From:GIANT   JW    Number    :00001
          Chris Atkinson        John Walker
Title:Design health facilities                    Change Issue:HEALTH
Contract/PO:CON To:DESIGN   From:GIANT   No:DES-91-00120Dated     :28AUG91
                                                  Required    :23AUG91
Reference  :   To:DESIGN   From:GIANT   No:00001     Status   :APP

Your costs are approved for the additional design services for the
following scope of work:

Provisions for a fitness and health facility. Facilities would include a
weight room, exercise room, men and womens locker rooms, a
raquetball court and a squash court.

                    Design costs ...........$ 10,000.00
                    Design time ............. 3 weeks
                    Construction time........ 4 weeks


Approved Date:28AUG91                        Cost:  $    10000.00
                                                              ▶
Commands: Add Codes Del Edit Find Generate Help Issue Print Ret Sort View Wndw
Windows : Approval  Costing  Description  Summary
```

Change Orders

```
ALL     :Material/To/From    MATERIALS DELIVERY                 DSGN

Material Name :ARCDRF   PO To:DESIGN   From:DESIGN   No.:EXPENSES
Material Title:Architectural Drafting              Spec Section:
Ordered From  :DESIGN      Delivered To:DESIGN      Req Item No.:

                Total Cost      Quantity    Units       Unit Cost

Contract    :$     14400.00    1200.00   Hrs       $       12.000
Amendment   :$         0.00       0.00             $        0.000
Delivered   :$      2400.00     200.00   First Delivery:12FEB92
Not Required:$      2400.00     200.00   Final Delivery:
Balance     :$     12000.00    1000.00   Activity ID   :

Recd      Quantity      Location      Ticket   Description Req Date   Remark

12FEB92        80.00 TDG-12STR               Drafting
19FEB92       120.00 TDG-12STR               Drafting




                                                              ▶
Commands: Add Codes Del Edit Find Help Issue More Print Ret Sort View Zoom
```

Materials Delivery

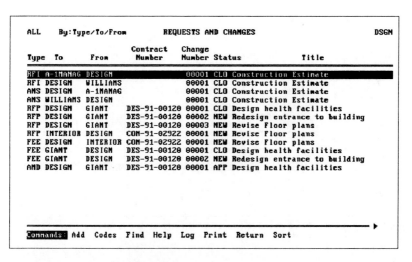

```
Sorted By:Cost Code              COST WORKSHEET                        DSGN
                                              DESIGN FEE
  Cost Code    |Original |Approved  |Revised    |Pending   |Estimated |Adjust-
  and Title    |Design Fee|Revisions|Design Fee |Revisions |Revisions |ments
 CONTINGENCY    24000.00|    0.00|   24000.00|    0.00|    0.00|    0.00|
 Misc. costs
 PHAS ADMM  G |  50000.00|    0.00|   50000.00|    0.00|    0.00|    0.00|
 Administration for all Phases
 PHAS SCHD  G |  15000.00|    0.00|   15000.00|    0.00|    0.00|    0.00|
 Scheduling all Phases
 PHAS SCHD  M |   5000.00|    0.00|    5000.00|    0.00|    0.00|    0.00|
 Scheduling Software
 PHAS SUPR  G |  65000.00|    0.00|   65000.00|    0.00|    0.00|    0.00|
 Supervision for all Phases
 PHAS SUPR  M |  10000.00|    0.00|   10000.00|    0.00|    0.00|    0.00|
 Contract Administration Software
 PHS1 BREP  S |   2500.00|    0.00|    2500.00|    0.00|    0.00|    0.00|
 Boring Report
 PHS1 BRNG  S |   3500.00|    0.00|    3500.00|    0.00|    0.00|    0.00|
 Borings in field
 Commands: Add Codes Delete Edit Find Help coLumns Open Print Return Sort Totals
```

Cost Worksheet

```
ALL    By:Type/To/From       REQUESTS AND CHANGES                    DSGN
                        Contract  Change
 Type  To       From    Number    Number Status          Title
 RFI A-1MANAG DESIGN               00001 CLO Construction Estimate
 RFI DESIGN   WILLIAMS             00001 CLO Construction Estimate
 AMS DESIGN   A-1MANAG             00001 CLO Construction Estimate
 AMS WILLIAMS DESIGN               00001 CLO Construction Estimate
 RFP DESIGN   GIANT     DES-91-00120 00001 CLO Design health facilities
 RFP DESIGN   GIANT     DES-91-00120 00002 NEW Redesign entrance to building
 RFP DESIGN   GIANT     DES-91-00120 00003 NEW Revise Floor plans
 RFP INTERIOR DESIGN    CON-91-02922 00001 NEW Revise Floor plans
 FEE DESIGN   INTERIOR  CON-91-02922 00001 NEW Revise Floor plans
 FEE GIANT    DESIGN    DES-91-00120 00001 CLO Design health facilities
 FEE GIANT    DESIGN    DES-91-00120 00002 NEW Redesign entrance to building
 AMD DESIGN   GIANT     DES-91-00120 00001 APP Design health facilities
 Commands: Add  Codes  Find  Help  Log  Print  Return  Sort
```

Request for Changes

```
Sorted By:Trans Date        LETTER OF  TRANSMITTAL                    DSGN
To  : GIANT     JW   Trans No.: 00001  Date  : 20AUG91  From: DESIGN    CA
Attn: John Walker                      Signed: Chris Atkinson
Giant Corporation                      The Design Group
300 Executive Parkway                  1215 Ventnor Avenue

King of Prussia        PA    19000     Philadelphia        PA    19000

Ref : Design Kick-off Meeting
      Office Building Project

Sent: X Attached     _ Separate Cover Via:
Item: _ Shop Dwg     _ Prints _ Plans        _ Samples   _ Specifications
      _ Letter       _ Change Order         X Other: Meeting Minutes
Action
  _ For Approval     X For Review & Comment  _ Returned For Corrections
  _ For Your Use     _ Approved As Submitted _ Resubmit  0 Copies For Approval
  _ As Requested     _ Approved As Noted     _ Submit    0 Copy For Distribution
  _ Bid Due:         _ Returned After Loan   _ Return    0 Copies Corrected Print
Copies To
FILE;ARCHDEPT;A-1MANAG;STRTDEPT;MECHDEPT;ELECDEPT;


Commands: Add Codes Del Edit Find Generate Help Issue Print Ret Sort View Wndw
Windows : Action  Items
```

Transmittal Letter

```
                          FORM LETTER                              DSGN
To:             Letter No.: LT-0003 Title: Outstanding Proposals
                                    Ref: Giant Corporation
                                         2600 Market Street
                                         Philadelphia
Salutation:
                  ═══════════ LEADING  PARAGRAPH ═══════════
            We have not received your proposal concerning the embedded
            conduit in the C.I.P. retaining wall at sections 9-A.


                  ═══════════ TRAILING PARAGRAPH ═══════════
            We need your estimates in writing no later than Wednesday of
            next week to avoid further delays to our concrete contractor.



Close: Very truly yours,          Company: ACME General Contractors
By   : Steve Johnson              Title  : Project Manager
CC   :
Typed: SRJ/jj                     Enclose:

Commands: Add  Delete  Edit  Find  Help  Print  Return
```

Dunning Letter

```
                              2600 Market Street
                            Philadelphia PA  19104
                               (215) 345-3293

                            MINUTES OF MEETING No.    2
                              May 15, 1992  8:02 AM
Project : Office Building               Job: 92C00015      Page:   1
Location: Stresson's Trailer            Subject: Progress Meeting

Here      Attendee                      Representing
Y/N Initials  Name                      Name

  Y    JS   James Strout           Aztec Engineering
  Y    SG   Stanley Green          Old Forge Ironworkers
  Y    AW   Al Wilson              Stresson Industrials
  Y    MA   Michael Austin         Stresson Industrials
  Y    MW   Mary Wilson            Stresson Industrials
  Y    LS   Louie Simpson          Testing USA, Inc.

Item    Description                           Status  Opened   Due   BIC

000001  Al stressed the need to get the submittals   NEW    20MAY92        JS
        submitted as soon as possible. Aztec
        engineering is late and promised to submit
        by 20MAY92

000002  Oldforge asked about getting a bigger        AOK    16MAY92        AW
        laydown area and an area to form the rebar
        on site. Al said he would ask ACME.

000003  Oldforge doesn't have electricity to their   NEW    16MAY92        AW
        trailer yet and wanted to know where they
        could run their lines. Al will find out
        by tomorrow morning.

000004  Al reminded everyone of the safety tool box  AOK                   SG
        meeting which will be held next week.
        A designated person from each subcontractor
        will be responsible for their company's
        safety program. This week Oldforge will
        talk about safety tips around rebar.

000005  The policy of handling RFI's were discussed. AOK
        Al will be responsible for getting answers
        to RFIs from ACME who will contact the
        designer.
```

With Primavera's Expedition meeting minutes can be printed to summarize each business item and show its current status, date it was first brought up, and who is responsible for taking action.

As you can see from this list of documents, using a computer can help you stay on top of all the issues facing a project manager today. As time goes on, you will wonder how you ever got along without one.

C4 STUDIO©. Modeled with Form•Z, rendered with StudioPro

Visualization Design Tools: 3D Modeling

hen was the last time you walked into a meeting with your client, floor plan in one hand and display boards with finishing building materials in the other hand? You sat with the client; rolled out your design development floor plans, elevations, and sections; and began to explain where the wall covering, ceiling tiles, and other finish materials would go in the finished building. The client either gazed at you with a blank face or blindly agreed with you. Computer technology will make this scenario obsolete. Why not use the computers that your architects are drafting on, in combination with visualization software, to create 3D computer models, photorealistic renderings, and animation walkthroughs that *show* your client how the volumetric space would look with the selected finished building materials, displayed in photographic quality?

With a combination of applications available for the Macintosh and IBM PC-compatible platforms today, the designer can fully involve the client in the design process through the use of 3D models and interactive walkthrough animation. During the design development stage of a project, through the use of what-if scenarios and instantaneous on-screen feedback, communication among everyone involved in the design can be greatly improved while enhancing the decision-making process.

Computer modeling allows designer and client to see the project in a whole new light. Now, when I say see, I _mean_ see – not squint, bend or imagine. You can see and experience your design as it develops and as it is intended to turn out.

Designers have always conceived their designs in three dimensions. Going back to the Renaissance period, perspective drawing was the primary means through which designers communicated their ideas. However, designers had to draw a new perspective each time they wanted to show a different view. Now, with the advent of three-dimensional (3D) visualization software, the model of a project only has to be drawn once. After that, the number of perspective views are unlimited. This means that the design can be analyzed from vantage points unavailable through traditional means.

BEFORE YOU BUY

Before your firm ventures to purchase a 3D modeling application, it is important to have a few facts straight. There are several modeling applications that are capable of representing 3D design spaces and forms. The 3D modeling application that you choose will depend on your type of practice and your budget. There are "designated" modeling applications that only provide the end user with modeling tools, and there is other 3D modeling software that also includes rendering and animation tools.

Designated Modeling Applications

The designated modeling applications are usually the best modeling applications on the market. These companies have spent all of their time designing an application that can model almost any physical form, and have done a great job doing so. On the other hand, companies that have developed software applications that include 3D modeling, rendering, and animation tools have done an incomplete job developing them. For example, the rendering environment may be quite exceptional, while the 3D modeling and animation tools are quite lacking. However, it is important to note that creating such applications is not in itself a bad practice, it just means that you as a designer must identify your firm's needs.

Applications that are capable of building sophisticated 3D models cannot be learned overnight. Like CADD, staff has to be trained to use these applications. Therefore, unless you want to spend hours of unproductive time flipping through the manuals trying to learn the modeling application, make sure that the developer or one of its associated companies either offer on-site training or some form of training aid such as video-tape tutorials that demonstrate the effective use of the software.

With the number of modeling applications on the market, it can be very difficult to choose. Some modeling applications were created for industrial designers who concentrate on product design, others for illustrators and still others for broadcast graphic designers. All these applications claim to have the capability to model architectural forms, and to some extent it can be done. You just have to exercise some care in making your choice and choose the product that most closely matches your practice.

Some 3D modelers also include a drafting module for 2D drawing. This is an invaluable tool for designers, since most 3D forms are generated from 2D shapes when extrusion and lathing functions are applied. In addition, the drafting environment has its own set of tools for producing fully accurate construction documents generated from the 3D model developed in the conceptual and design development stages of the design project.

As an architect, interior designer, urban planner, landscape designer, or engineer, you want a design tool that speaks your language, that is capable of handling every facet of your project. You want a modeling application that can create an unlimited assortment of 3D objects; a tool that can generate accurate 3D forms either graphically or through numeric inputs that define points relative to cartesian planes or planes generated somewhere in 3D space.

Designers of the built environment seldom design the skeleton of a structure alone. Custom details and ornaments have to be designed and analyzed. 3D computer modeling gives designers the ability to perform this task right in the office. Interior designers and landscape architects need a tool that will also give them the freedom and flexibility to design furniture, lighting, sculpture, and signage. After all, the designer already knows the mindset of the client and what kind of image needs to be projected in the final design. Why not use your modeling tool to design and visualize a complete project? Look for a modeling design tool that has been developed for a designer like yourself, that is capable of generating, manipulating and sculpting objects three dimensionally – a tool that speaks a language that you understand.

3D MODELING FEATURES

Original

Basically there are two types of 3D modeling applications: surface and solid. Surface modelers generate shapes by their membrane and have a 2D character. They have no volume; rather, they are used as a base to generate 3D forms. A surface object can be a simple open or closed line or a meshed surface. On the other hand, a solid modeler generates well-formed enclosed objects that have 3D characteristics. Solid modeling is sometimes characterized by a group of innovative functions called boolean tools (union, intersection, and difference) that are applied to solids in order to create complex design forms.

Union

Intersection

Difference
"B" from "A"

Difference
"A" from "B"

The *union tool* derives a single object from the union of two objects or volumes; the *intersection tool* creates an object from the intersection of two objects or volumes; the *difference tool* derives an object from the difference of two surfaces or volumes. For designers of the built environment, solid modelers are often the natural choice because they more closely conform to the manner in which structures are assembled, piece by piece (foundation, walls, roof, partitions, and so on ...) in the real world. However, good design incorporates both surface and solid forms to create an environment, so choose a 3D modeler that includes both surface and solid modeling techniques. 3D modeling applications use many tools to create 3D forms from 2D planes, contours, and shapes. Some of these tools are explained below.

Spline-based and *NURBS (nonuniform rational B-spline)*

These modeling techniques use spline curves to create smooth, curved, organic, and geometric forms. This style of modeling allows the designer to push and pull on points to reshape elements of the 3D model into its intended visual appearance. It is excellent for modeling sophisticated architectural structures such as Pompidou Center in France, the Hong Kong Bank in Hong Kong, and the Lloyds of London renovation/expansion in London.

LATHING:

This function allows the designer to create 3D shapes of circular symmetry, by first drawing the 2D profile and then revolving the profile 360 degrees about the z axis.

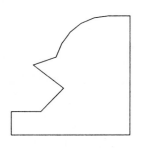 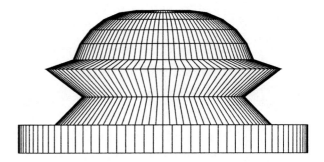

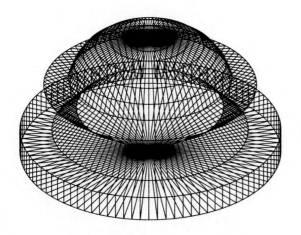

This section of the book attempts to dismantle the myth that computer visualization designing is difficult. As you can see, the super dome, like many forms, is a very symmetrical structure; therefore, once the dimensions are verified, only its 2D profile needs to be drawn and then revolved about the z-axis.

SWEEP SURFACING:

This function allows the designer to create solid 3D shapes by sweeping a 2D source shape along a path .

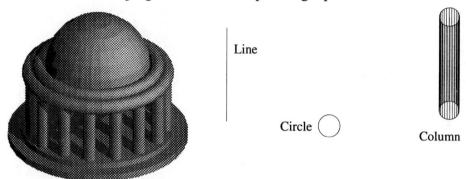

Line

Circle

Column

In this example each of the columns was created by first drawing the circumference of the column; then a line perpendicular to the reference plane was drawn. Using the sweep modeling tool the circle was then swept along the path of the line to create the column.

EXTRUSION:

This function gives depth to 2D shapes and objects. For example, the walls of a floor plan are extruded to illustrate a sense of space and volume.

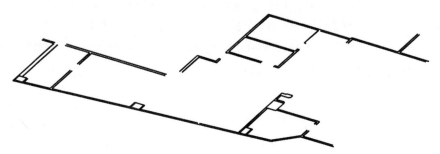

Floor plan before extrusion.

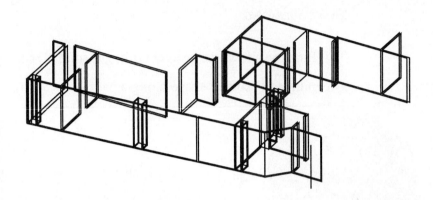

Floor plan after extrusion.

If this were a class, your instructor would have said at this point that these three tools provide the foundation of 3D Computer Visualization 101 (lathe/revolve, sweep surfacing, and extrusion). Now go forth, get some of your past designs, apply these principles, and practice, practice, practice.

Since most 3D shapes and forms can be derived from 2D shapes, it is important that modeling applications allow the designer to work in both two and three dimensions. This is a very constructive feature because while drawing in 2D, the designer can maintain 3D views of what the final model will look like. As a result, adjustments can be made on the fly.

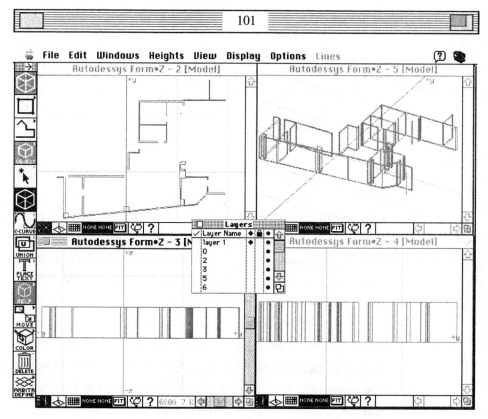

... it is important that modeling applications allow the designer to design in both two and three dimensions.

2D DESIGN VISUALIZATION

With all the interest in 3D modeling applications, it is easy to forget that there are firms that, because of the nature of their design practice, depend on software applications that are specifically developed for 2D conceptual design. These applications are intended to help designers lay out physical space relationships during the design development phase through a set of tools that gives freedom to place architectural elements such as walls, doors, windows, beams, and columns.

These applications are also equipped with basic facility management functions; standard architectural notation symbols such as detail and section; and cells (diagrammatic images) for electrical, plumbing, and HVAC.

For complex institutional projects such as prisons, health care facilities, civic centers, court houses, and universities, these visualization tools are used during the design development phase to lay out single-line spatial relationships and zoning diagrams to scale. Once approved, these single-lined, scaled diagrams can quickly be transformed into double-lined floor plans. These applications provide the designer with tools that will allow the placement of doors, windows, and other architectural symbols. If architectural attributes of the floor plan are given 3D characters, then you can transform the 2D plan into a 3D model for volumetric studies.

INDISPENSABLE TOOLS

For architects, urban planners, and landscape designers, having a 3D computer model of the proposed site during the initial stage of a design project gives you the ability to visualize the landform, thereby analyzing the best location for the building's footprint. Whether your firm is applying traditional methods or using a computer application, site modeling and analysis have always been a tedious but necessary part of the design process.

High-end 3D modelers have begun to incorporate a *terrain tool* that makes these design studies easy to carry out. The *terrain modeler* allows the designer to either draw the 2D contours of the site directly onto the computer or scan the image of the site, and then trace the contours. Once this graphic data is in its correct location, you simply enter the height between the contours, then with the terrain tool selected, click on each contour line – from lowest to highest – and you have your contour map. The terrain modeler also gives the option of viewing the site as a mesh, stepped, or triangulated contour model.

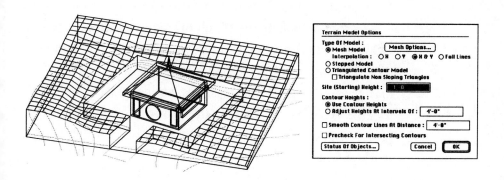

In this example the contour map of the site was digitized into the computer. Within Autodessys' form•Z, the terrain modeling dialog was accessed, contour heights set, and the site model constructed. From this site model we were able to place the model of the proposed at different locations until the most appropriate one was found. All these design visualization studies were done on the computer–at a fraction of the time it takes to conduct traditional studies.

Another design task that the computer has revolutionized is that of *sun study analysis*. It is very important to understand how sun will affect the design of your structure or landform. Will your structure receive direct sunlight throughout the day? What impact will this occurrence have on the design of the HVAC system? Will the structure be shaded by adjacent buildings? If there is a courtyard or common space, will it be shaded, or will it receive sunlight — especially during the cold months of the year? Will the openings in the proposed structure need specially designed overhangs or screens? All these concerns must be addressed when designing a structure, an urban development, or a landscaped park.

Many design firms still use sundials as a means of estimating the manner in which the sun will affect a design. However, this system is quite inaccurate. 3D computer modelers are now providing designers with a *sun study analysis tool* to make this task less labor-intensive. With this tool the designer can analyze the behavior of the sun and its effect on the design of the proposed site, anywhere in the world, and at any time.

Geographic Position

Abidjan, Ivory Coast
Abu Zaby, United Arab Emirates
Acapulco, Mexico
Adana, Turkey
Addis Ababa, Ethiopia
Adelaide, Australia
Aden, Yemen : South
Agra, India
Ahmadabad, India

List By :
● City
○ Country

Add...
Edit...
Delete
‹None›

City : ‹None›
Latitude :
Longitude :
Time Zone :

Cancel
OK

Add City

Country : Trinidad and Tobago
City : ‹New City›
Latitude : 0° 0' N
Longitude : 0° 0' E
Time Zone : 12:00

Cancel
OK

You can select cities and
countries from the hundreds listed.

If the city or country is not included,
and you know the longitude and latitude
of your site, the application would fill in
the city and country so you can
conduct sun studies.

Sun

Site Location : ‹None›

Choose Site...   Angle Of Site North : 90°

┌─Date & Time─────────────────────────
Month : November   Day Of Month : 24
Time : 12:19   ● A.M ○ P.M   ☐ Daylight Savings

Summer Solstice   Vernal Equinox   Current Time
Winter Solstice   Autumnal Equinox

Sun Altitude : 34.12°   Cancel
Sun Azimuth : 67.14°   From : South   OK

An indispensable design tool included in Autodessys' Form•Z modeling application gives
designers the ability to conduct sun studies for anywhere in the world at any time of the
day, 365 days per year.

In addition, these high-end modeling applications
also have the capability to animate the sun's path over your
proposed site from sunrise to sunset. What a tool! This is an
indispensable tool for designers of forms, spaces, and structures
in the built environment.

When the sun analysis tool is used in conjunction with animation tools, designers can instantaneously see what positive or negative effects the path of the sun will have on the design of the proposed structure, thereby making the necessary design adjustments. This feature will also give designers the advantage of seeing whether other neighboring structures will cast shadows on the new building, or whether the new building will cast unnecessary or beneficial shadows on adjacent structures. These two tools are vital in the design of energy-efficient buildings and spaces. If you think the tools discussed can improve your firm's productivity,then be sure to purchase a modeling application that offers these features.

CASE STUDY

Project: Two-story church sanctuary to accommodate 2500 persons seated in the main as well as balcony area.

Client: Ebenezer A.M.E. Church,
            Ft. Washington, MD

Consultant: C4 STUDIO,

BACKGROUND

We were approached to do this job because the client had difficulty grasping the intent of the 2D drawings, and wanted, very much, to experience the design in three dimensions. Also, neither the architectural nor the interior design firm offered computer visualization services within their scope of practice.

Using Form•Z to construct the model, the importance of computer visualization in design decision making for designers as well as clients was quite clear. What can also make this design approach natural to designers is the fact that constructing a computer model follows the same format as constructing a structure. You begin with a floor, add vertical structural members that are supported horizontally, add the roof, enclose the structure and add interior and exterior finishes and furniture.

Let's take a look!

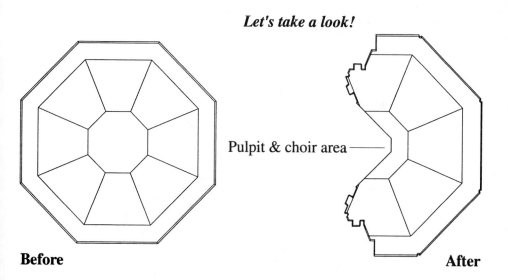

Pulpit & choir area ——

Before

After

As in the construction of a structure, there is no room for waste. Since we knew that the contour of the sanctuary would begin to slope up at the pulpit area and the area below was not going to be occupied, the floor was 'trimmed and stitched'.

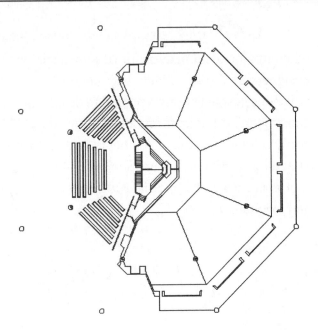

Pulpit and choir loft added.

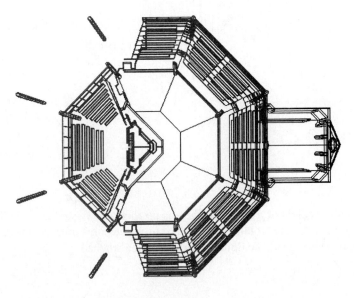

Balcony and wall enclosures added.

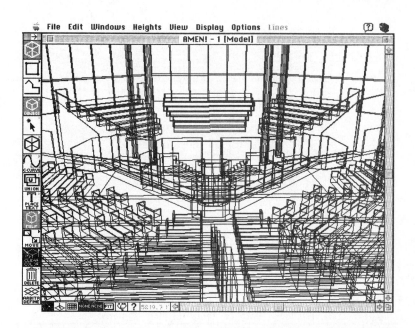

Interior perspectives showing seating configuration, pulpit and choir area.

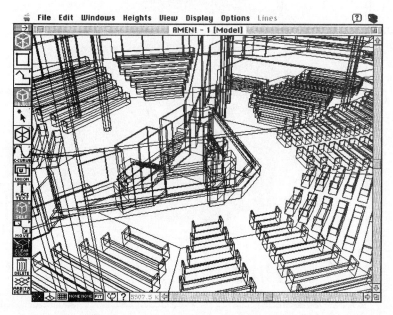

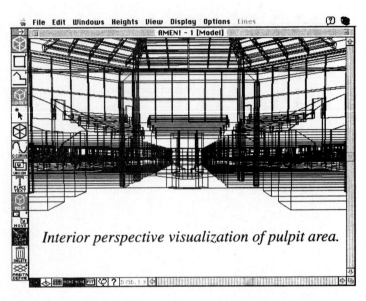

Interior perspective visualization of pulpit area.

Putting it all together!

C4 STUDIO©, Modeled with Form•Z, rendered with StudioPro

VISUALIZATION
DESIGN TOOLS:
COMPUTER RENDERING

nce the 3D model is complete, it is time to prepare for rendering. You can either apply the actual textures or use colors to represent surfaces, depending on the quality you want to achieve. Rendering on the computer differs from conventional rendering in that the computer is quicker and much more flexible. Rendering is the action that begins to add life to your model. At this stage, viewpoints and camera angles are determined, light sources are added and positioned, and additional details such as textures that represent different building materials, furniture, trees, shrubs, people, and shadows are all added in order to breathe life into the 3D model.

Unlike the presentation techniques discussed earlier, computer rendering is presented here as a tool that aids designers in confirming form, function, building materials, and finishes. Regardless of your design discipline, it is important to analyze the 3D model, complete with the proposed finish materials mapped onto the respective surfaces. Analyses (such as do the colors clash; are the proposed finishes conveying the desired ambiance; should alternative materials be considered) are just a few of the many questions that designers are confronted with during the design development stage of a project.

This degree of analysis may arise either during interoffice meetings or meetings with the client. By integrating computer rendering techniques, interior and exterior building materials and finishes can be applied to the 3D model and alternatives can be studied and finalized during design meetings. This method is quicker and less expensive than traditional rendering techniques. It also makes more sense for several reasons. First, the designer has more control over the quality and schedule since the rendering will be done in-house, on the computer-created 3D model – thereby integrating the design process. Secondly, once the model is rendered, the design team and client have the ability to study the project from vantage points that assist in making appropriate design decisions.

THE PROCESS

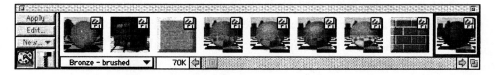

ADDING SURFACES:

Texture mapping is one of the processes used to apply surface properties to a 3D model. Through this process, 3D models develop character when various image files are placed on the surfaces of each object in the model.

Many rendering applications can be purchased with hundreds of PICT image files that represent building materials and finishes, ready to be used on 3D models. In an instance when a designer chooses a finish material that is not represented in the rendering application's image file library, a sample of that building material can be scanned into the computer using a high quality flat-bed scanner.

The resulting file can be saved as either a PICT, TIFF, TARGA, or GIF image file, ready to be mapped onto surfaces of the model. Whether it is carpet, wall covering, wood, acoustical ceiling, or paving, any type of building material or finish can be scanned and used as an image file for rendering a 3D model.

Procedural mapping is another process used to apply surface properties to 3D models. This is a process in which the computer creates texture properties through mathematical functions. Once these textures are applied to an object, forms appear as though they were molded from blocks of real materials. For example, once an image is applied and rendered properly, it is very difficult to tell the difference between a photograph and computer-generated materials such as wood or marble.

The realism of a 3D model can be accomplished when certain properties of textures, such as reflectiveness, transparency, refraction, and bump mapping (employing dark and light values to represent the bumps in real building materials), are manipulated. In addition, the manner in which textures are mapped onto forms must be performed precisely. For example, *cylindrical mapping* should be used to apply textures onto forms such as columns; *spherical mapping*, for applying textures to forms such as domes; *cubic mapping*, for mapping textures onto multiple-sided forms, and *planar mapping* for mapping textures onto flat surfaces.

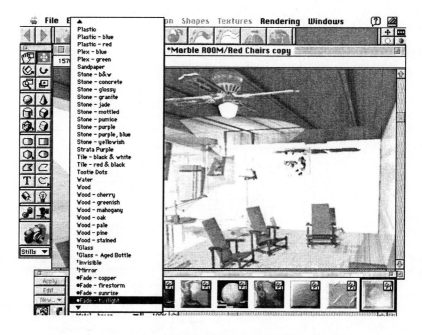

Rendering applications like StrataVision's StudioPro, Pixar's Renderman, Autodesk 3D Studio and CrystalGraphics Topas Professional give the designer access to an abundance of textures that are used to represent building materials and finishes.

StudioPro's *texture editing dialog box* gives the designer the ability to access the color palette and change the color of the material/texture, as well as view a preview before accepting the new texture into the model. For further enhancement, designers also have access to the *expert dialog box*.

Once you have selected a texture or expert editing, you can then adjust the material's reflectivity, smoothness, transparency, glow factor, diffusion and bump amplitude.

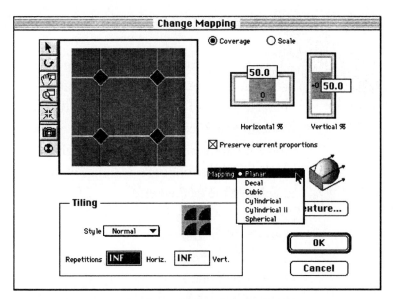

Once you have selected a texture, it is important that not only the material be scaled appropriately, but that you select the correct type of plane (cubic, planar, spherical ...) in order to secure accurate texture mapping.

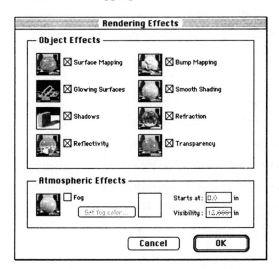

Almost all rendering applications present the designer with a dialog box with a variety of choices to customize the rendering effects of the design. It is important to note that the more effects you select, the longer the model will take to render.

USING LIGHT TO DEFINE THE MODEL

Once the textures are added to the 3D model, lighting is applied in order to define depth and emphasize the characteristics of all textures mapped onto the model. Most modeling applications incorporate some combination of ambient, spot, point, and directional light sources. The intensity and color of each one of these light sources can be manipulated to achieve the desired effect.

Ambient light source:
This type of lighting has no origin; it exists throughout the environment. Ambient lighting is nondirectional and has uniform intensity everywhere. When activated, this general illumination fills shaded or shadowed areas of a model so that details not directly illuminated by other light sources are still visible. Most of these applications present the designer with the opportunity to adjust the color and hue, luminance, and saturation values (HLS) of the light source.

Spotlight source:
Spotlighting points in a specific direction and is used to highlight a defined space, form, or element within the 3D model. The designer will be able to manipulate the spotlight's illumination parameters such as cone angle, the focus (how quickly the spotlight beam drops off), the intensity, distance above the object, and shadows that will be cast.

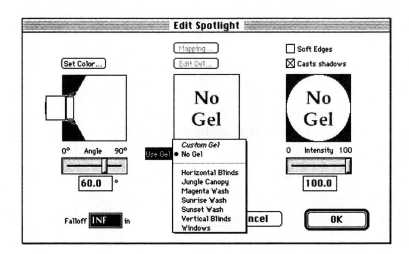

Set spotlight color. Set the desired angle of the spotlight. Set spotlight intensity. Add special lighting effects through a variety of gels (horizontal blinds, windows ...)

Point light source:

Similar to a light bulb, point light sources dissipate light in all directions. As described in the following diagrams, illumination parameters can also be manipulated to achieve the desired ambiance.

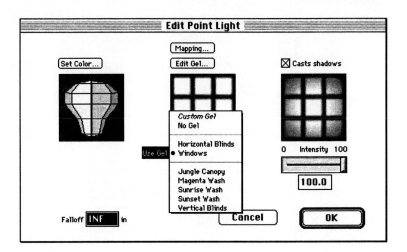

Set point light color. Set the desired angle of the point light. Set point light intensity. Add special lighting effects through a variety of gels (horizontal blinds, windows ...)

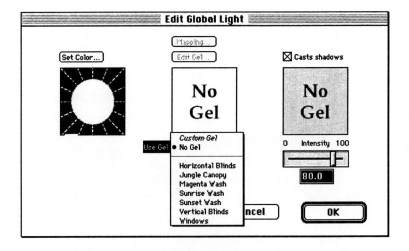

Set global light color. Set the desired angle of the global light. Set global light intensity. Add special lighting effects through a variety of gels (horizontal blinds, windows ...)

Directional light source:

Directional lighting acts as a global source and is designed to illuminate the entire 3D model like sunlight striking the earth. As discussed previously, many visualization applications possess the added ability of manipulating directional lighting to simulate sunlight for any time, date, and location.

Although the light sources discussed above improve the definition of your 3D model, the more light sources you add, the longer the rendering time. In addition, casting shadows significantly increase the rendering time, depending on the size of the area the shadow is cast upon and the shadow parameter setting.

RENDERING ENGINE

Once light sources and camera angles have been finalized, designers are faced with the option of using several rendering techniques to illustrate design solutions.

To get a basic feel for spatial relationships within the 3D model, designers can use *flat, or gouraud,* rendering techniques on the wire-frame of the model. A wire-frame has a mesh appearance and is the quickest and simplest way of viewing a 3D model. Flat rendering begins to add a visible skin to the model, applying a single color to each form. Gouraud rendering goes a step further in defining the smooth surfaces of each object in the 3D model and illustrates the lighting.

For more detailed representation of spaces, forms, and objects in the 3D model, *phong shading, ray tracing* and *RenderMan* rendering techniques should be used. The two latter have the capability to produce photorealistic images.

Of these three types of rendering techniques, phong shading is the fastest. As you progress from phong shading to RenderMan and ray tracing, the quality of the image and the level of complex forms in the model become much more pronounced. For instance, when a 3D model is rendered using ray tracing or RenderMan techniques, the resulting images, surfaces, and objects are given photorealistic properties. You could actually see wood grains, brick contours, fabric textures, glass and reflective surfaces, realistic reflections, and shadows created from one or a combination of light sources.

Designers wanting a more artistic appearance for their 3D model can use a rendering technique called RayPainting. When this technique is activated, the resulting 3D model will take on either an Art Deco, chalk, crackled, dry brush, fur, pencil, Seraut, soft oil, Van Gogh, or watercolor appearance.

Let's Render

Unlike human beings, computers do not require sleep. Since the cost of electricity is less expensive at night you can use your computers in this way to become productive 24 hours a day.

If you have a small design practice and do not have your computers networked to each other, reap the benefits of your investment and set your model to render overnight before you leave the office. You can even queue your different views of the model for renderings, one after the other. If you have a very powerful computer, the rendered images might be ready for viewing next morning. If your model is not finished rendering, you can suspend the rendering, and resume later.

With the development of various local area network systems, a new concept in rendering has been created on the computer that is an alternative to the above scenario. This process is called distributive rendering. Through this system, a host computer distributes the rendering job over a network of computers linked together. Each computer on the network is charged with completing a portion of the rendering, and once completed, its segment of the job is sent back to the host computer for assembly - decreasing total rendering time.

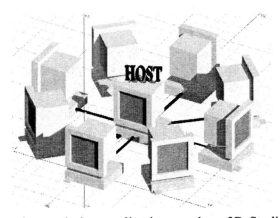

All the major rendering applications such as 3D Studio, Topas Professional, StudioPro and RenderMan, allow distributive rendering over a network.

There are three ways in which distributive rendering can be accomplished. First, the rendering application is installed on the host computer. Then you purchase a separate rendering engine module (not to be confused with the entire rendering application), one for each computer attached to the network. The host then distributes portions of the job to the rendering engines on each of the network computers. Other software applications offer an alternative solution. Here, you only purchase one copy of the rendering software application, to be installed on the host computer as well as the network computers to achieve the same goal of distributive rendering. The software developers grant you a license that allows for legal installation on multiple machines solely for the purpose of distributing the task of rendering. This approach represents a significant cost savings.

Rendering productivity now becomes a function of how many computers are connected to the network and the speed at which images are transported over the network. In addition, the more powerful the computers, the larger the hard drives, and the greater the amount of memory available (RAM), the more productive your rendering process will be.

A third method of distributing rendering is to have multiple computers in one. Let me explain: many companies are developing accelerator cards/boards that once installed either have an additive effect on the computer's processing power or take over the processing functions entirely.

Having multiple accelerator boards working within your computer can significantly decrease the rendering time when compared to a network system, because information does not have to travel over a network - all the rendering work is done at a single workstation using multiple processor cards.

It is important to note that any of the distributive rendering approaches used will still allow you to maintain maximum productivity since each system has the ability to render in the background while allowing you to perform the other tasks discussed in this book.

Let us take a look at some examples of computer rendered models. Note how the materials, lights and shadows produce photorealistic quality images.

Marble Room (StrataVision's StudioPro) ©1993 C4 STUDIO

Ebenezer A.M.E. Church (Modeled in Autodessys' Form•Z and rendered with Electric Image Animation) ©1994 C4 STUDIO

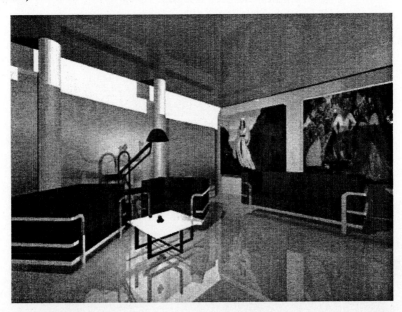

Office lobby (Modeled in Autodessys' Form•Z and rendered with StrataVision's StudioPro) ©1994 C4 STUDIO

POSTRENDERING EDITING

Once the renderings of your 3D model are completed, they can be imported into image editing applications where they can be enhanced and retouched and objects not added during the modeling or rendering stages can be incorporated. For example, whenever you are under a deadline (which is probably always), but still want to present the photorealistic quality of your design, you can render the model with all the rendering attributes turned on except the shadow and reflection functions. When the rendering is completed, open the file in an image editing application and use the editing and painting tools to apply shadows and reflective surfaces to the image. You have to remember that you are the one who is in control of the computer, and understanding how to manipulate your software applications and hardware will be the key to greater office productivity.

Even though ray tracing and RenderMan rendering techniques produce photoquality images that illustrate real characteristics of building materials and finishes, designers have continued to cling to their artistic side. Many have complained that photorealistically rendered images, have a very "computerish, high-tech look." This is an additional reason why image editing applications are indispensable tools to the designer. These applications allow you to apply artistic filters to your rendered 3D model. By applying filters, a 3D model can change its appearance to a watercolor, dry brush, emboss, fresco, mosaic, felt pen, crayon, airbrush, charcoal, colored pencil, rough pastel, or oil paint finish.

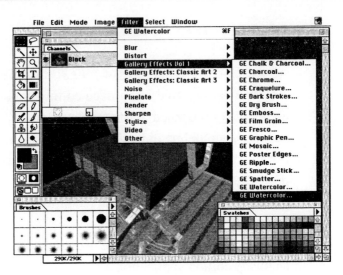

Using Adobe Photoshop, you can apply artistic filters such as watercolor, dry brush, emboss, fresco, mosaic, felt pen, crayon, airbrush, charcoal, colored pencil, rough pastel, or oil paint to a rendered image.

Image editing applications have also revolutionized the traditional practice of architectural photography. Traditionally, a photographer created a photomontage of a design project by first taking a photograph of the proposed site, then taking another photograph of the cardboard model of the project. In a photography lab the two photographs were then combined, to the approximate perspective of the site. Image editing applications have moved this extremely time consuming task from the hands of a specialist to the hands of the designer.

These digital photography labs allow the designer to import an image of the proposed site, using a scanning device, directly onto the computer screen. Once the image of the site is imported, the rendered 3D model can be incorporated and scaled to match the perspective of the proposed site. This means that multiple site composition and site contextual analysis can be included in the computer visualization design process. This process is less expensive and less time consuming than traditional methods. It also allows the client, designers, and consultants to view the proposed building in context with the site, thereby making accurate and well-communicated design decisions.

C4 STUDIO©, Modeled with Form•Z, rendered with StudioPro

ANIMATION

AS A

DESIGN TOOL

arlier, the concept of animation was briefly introduced. In this chapter we give a more detailed discussion of how animation can be used during the design and construction phase of a project.

As designers of the built environment, you are responsible for designing landforms, urban spaces, and interior and exterior building structures. These projects will be inhabited by people. These spaces and design forms will be experienced by the building's future occupants. Therefore, one should take all possible precautions to limit design errors which can result in inadequate or inappropriate design solutions. That is why designers, principals, consultants and clients (when necessary) should use animation as a design tool to experience the landforms, urban spaces, and interior and exterior building structures during the design and construction phase of a project.

However, before we get into the theory of animation, let us just look at a practical example of how this tool can be used in the formation of a design solution. For this example, let us look at the design of a church.

There is a great degree of order that goes into the design of a church. Ritual activities must flow in a carefully choreographed order. Once worshipers enter the grand entrances that lead to the vestibule, they are escorted in an orderly manner to their seats, so as not to interrupt the service in progress. Circulation paths to the lower or upper levels of the sanctuary must be clear. In addition, the design has to allow everyone a view of the presiding minister and vice versa. Any errors in the flow of activities can adversely affect the service. As the designer, you must determine how people get from point A to point B. So, you the designer must decide the most efficient and effective way for people to traverse throughout the sanctuary before, during and after the worship service. You need to design attractive entrances, points of interest, processional activities, preaching areas, sitting areas, viewing areas, and stairs to move from one level to another. All these are dynamic activities that cannot be adequately conveyed and analyzed with 2D drawings or a miniature cardboard model.

CASE STUDY

In the aforementioned example, we were initially hired to create a 3D model of the sanctuary area of this church, with a concentration on the pulpit and surrounding area from which the minister would preach. It is important to note that this service was purely for design analysis.

The client did not have a clear understanding of what the 3D volume of the sanctuary would look like by looking at the 2D plans. Sound familiar ? The pastor had specific visions of how he wanted the pulpit area to be perceived. Although these ideas were conveyed to the designers, it was difficult for the pastor to grasp this by looking at 2D drawings. Once the computer model was completed, the request to analyze views of the sanctuary other than the pulpit area became automatic, for the minister also had visions of how the sanctuary should be perceived from the pulpit area. Even though the still snapshot views were helpful for making critical design decisions, they did not convey the flow of dynamic activities that are conducted during the worship service. As a result, the scope of our job naturally expanded to the creation of animation sequences. While viewing the animation sequence of the project, several design flaws were noted and corrected. For example, the initial design had a central aisle that was perpendicular to the pulpit and directly in the line of vision of the minister.

During the animation sequence it was determined by the client, that this central aisle was a problem because during the service people would be going in and out of their seats. The minister pointed out that this would be a major distraction to him. Consequently, the decision was made to delete the central aisle and redesign the circulation flow within the sanctuary.

As the animation progressed from the front entrance to the pulpit area, it was also observed that the wall separating the pulpit area and the musician's area was obscuring the congregation's view of the musicians. The design team was left with two options - either lower the wall or, make the wall transparent. Here again, the animation pointed out a problem that was not easily recognizable to a layperson looking at a 2D plan. Until the animation sequence began, there was no appreciation by the client for the height of the wall or the fact that it was opaque.

Had these and other design problems not been pointed out during the animation design studies, the final structure would not have been as functionally or aesthetically pleasing to the ministerial staff and the congregation. In addition, it would have been too late to make such significant design and structural changes without incurring considerable expense. In this case, spending the money for the animation services saved several hundred thousand dollars in the construction phase. Using animation as a design analysis tool allows for interactive and immediate design decision making that can assist designers in exploring different design solutions, while still keeping the project within the agreed-upon budget, and most importantly deliver the finished project to the client on time.

HOW ANIMATION WORKS

When you create the 3D model of your design project, you have basically completed 50 percent of the task necessary to produce an animation sequence. Therefore, a well-constructed 3D model is a key ingredient in producing realistic 3D animation that allows the designer to experience and analyze the form, space, and structure of a design project.

Still images like the ones created using a camera are the basis for creating animation sequences. This is because the brain perceives a series of still images, displayed in rapid succession, as motion. Animation, therefore, is essentially a series of snapshots (frames) which, once recorded, are replayed at high speed to create the illusion of motion. The minimum speed at which the brain is able to captures pictures flowing together is somewhere between 12 and 30 frames per second. Therefore, a one-minute animation would have between 720 and 1800 separate frames or snapshots. The more frames per second, the smoother the illusion of motion, the fewer frames per second, the more the motion will appear abrupt and jolted. The beauty of creating animation sequences on the computer is that you do not have to create each of the 1800 frames for a one-minute animation. As the designer, you decide which are the critical snapshots or views in your design that you want to show, analyze or exemplify.

As you move through the 3D model taking snapshots, the computer and your animation application will define these views as *key frames*. Once these key frames are in place, the computer interpolates all views in between the key frames (the views between each snapshot) to create a motion path.

THE IDEAL ANIMATION DESIGN TOOL

Autodesk's 3D Studio provides designers with a product in which they have total control over the environment. You can take your model to places where no cardboard model could ever go. You can see your model from vantage points limited only by your imagination. 3D Studio provides you with a range of tools to accomplish your visualization and animation projects in style. It will facilitate better communication between designer and client, because you will be discussing the project from a point of view that the client will understand infinitely better than a 2D plan or a cardboard model. Unlike CAD, where the product is perceived as flat, static, and boring by the client, animation produces a living, motion-filled glimpse of the design that both the designer and client will find irresistible.

ANIMATION POWER TOOLS

CAMERA MANIPULATION

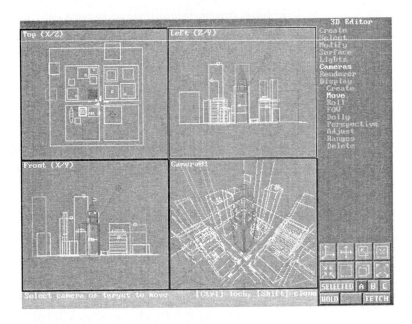

CAMERA MOVE TOOL

By first placing a camera in any of the 2D view-windows and then selecting the move command, the designer is able to move the camera in any of these three views and control how the design is experienced in real time in the 3D view-window. This is not just walking around a physical cardboard model. This tool gives the designer the opportunity to simulate dynamic elements such as pedestrian and vehicular circulation, scale, context, and aesthetics ... all in real time.

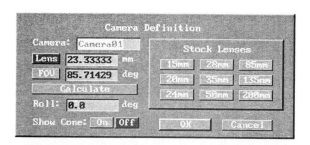

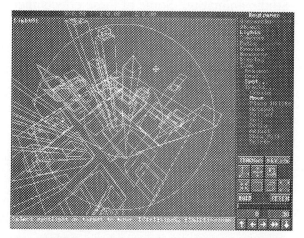

CAMERA PERSPECTIVE TOOL

One of the major pitfalls of traditional cardboard models has been the inability for someone to experience and have a true sense of the physical characteristics of the design. For example, in the case of the design of a city center, it is impossible for anyone to experience the true perspective of skyscrapers . There is no sense of being. However, by using the perspective tool in 3D Studio, the designer is able to interactively change the perspective for viewing the design by simply moving the mouse ... resulting in dynamic views for design analysis.

IPAS ROUTINES

IPAS routines are special effects developed by many third-party companies to *plug-in* to Autodesk's 3D Studio. The Yost Group has been in the forefront in this effort and has developed quite a few that will add interest to your 3D Studio animation. Some of these effects include snow, rain, explode, fireworks, and tornado. Another leader in this area is Schreiber Instruments who has developed an entire product line of 3D effects and objects. For instance, their *Architectpak* includes *Nursery* (trees), *Detailor*, *Lightpak* (outdoor lighting), *3D People*, and *Sun*.

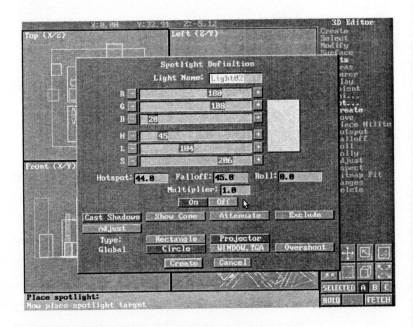

THE CONTROL OVER LIGHT
"SPOTLIGHT/DAYLIGHT"

This tool gives the designer the power to change the color of the lighting that will be present throughout your animation. You can apply the warm golden glow of a late summer light on a log cabin, or you can create the atmosphere of fluorescent lamps in an office. The cast shadow option will allow you to cast crisp rendered shadows over a model of any size. With this tool a spot (representing the sun) can be put over an entire city. The other options would give you further control of the spotlights in your animation.

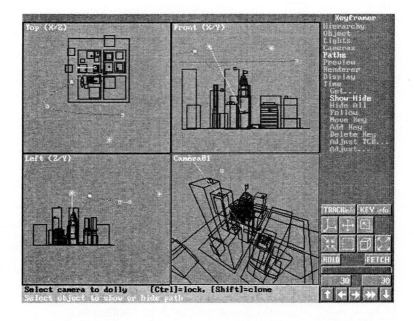

KEYFRAMER showing animation path.

POSTANIMATION EDITING:

ADOBE PREMIER AND MACROMIND DIRECTOR

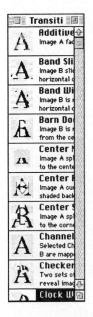

For those projects where a more polished presentation is required, postanimation editing products like Adobe's Premier will take your animation to the next level. In this digital studio, you can add sound overlays, insert sophisticated transitions between frames, mix still renderings with animated clips, add text overlays, and, in short, make your animation clip into a movie event.

Premier takes your animation and breaks it down into individual frames in a construction window. The construction window consists of tracks and a time line. There is a track for special effects, multiple tracks for video or still images, a track for superimposed text or graphics, and multiple audio tracks. Using the time line, you can lay out the audio so it starts at a specific frame and ends at another.

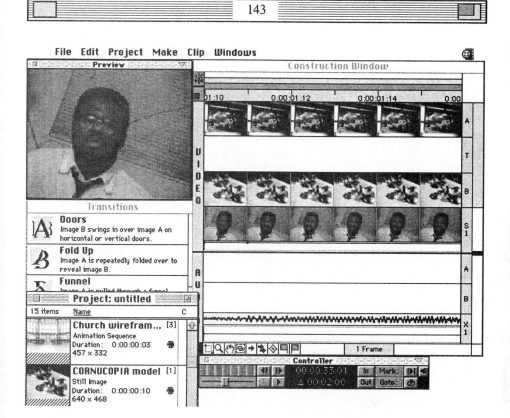

Adobe Premier's interface where animations are edited, and integrated with live video, audio, renderings and photography.

You can place special effects like wipes and fades between specific frames. You can create animated text overlays to create titles and credits that play over other clips. Your animation can be spliced with another one or with still images. You can also edit the animation by removing frames or changing their position in any way that suits your purposes. After you have finished, you are ready to compile your movie. Output options include "Quicktime " and "out to video". It really is like having a video lab on your desktop.

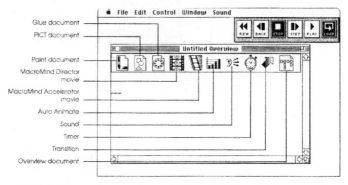

Macromind Director's overview window with icons that represent documents and effects.

If you have ever seen an on-line tutorial with animation, sound, video, and an interface that allows the user to interactively navigate through the tutorial, or run a demo disk of a particular software product, you have seen Macromind Director in action. It is a multimedia presentation tool that allows you to combine information from a variety of media sources - video, audio, and digital – to create your presentations. In addition, you can use "scripting" to bring interactivity to your presentation. The uses are many but, in our context, you can use it to do things like a digital resume, introducing your company and services to potential clients.

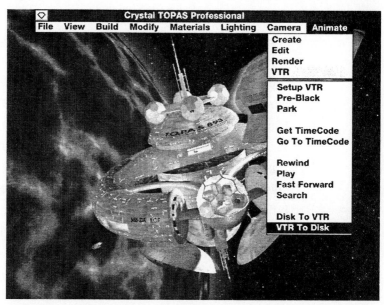

Crystal Topas allows you to download your animation from the computer to a video tape recorder (VTR) after editing is complete.

THE FUTURE OF ANIMATION IN DESIGN

Because our world is overpopulated, we have no choice but to build upon any available land. Whether the land is threatened by earthquakes, flooding, hurricanes, or the blazing desert sun, people are occupying these lands, not necessarily from choice, but from necessity. As designers, we have no control over the environment, but we do have access to information concerning the forces of nature. As such, we are better able to design structures that will withstand those forces and provide protection against the elements of nature.

Over the last few years scientist have collected and studied the behavior and destructive of earthquakes on the west coast of the United States, Mexico and more recently India. Meteorological experts have flown into the eye of storms in the southern states of the United States and in the Caribbean to collect data. In the midwestern states of the United States, we have witnessed flooding of unprecedented proportions, and scientists and researchers have collected and studied this natural disaster and its destructive effect on the built and natural environment. In the desert states of the Middle East and elsewhere, the blistering sun has continued to be a force to be reckoned with.

Working in conjunction with the scientists, the designers may someday create animation sequences of floods, hurricanes, and earthquakes to predict the potential consequences to structures and urban spaces. Algorithms to represent the scientific data on these natural disasters in a vector or coordinate format would have to be developed. Then, we could program into the animation, the equations and the resulting "morph" or change in position over time, that would occur for, say, a hurricane with winds of a certain speed or an earthquake registering x on the Richter scale. Animation routines based on physics, where snow is not just a visual effect, but actually has physical properties like weight, will result in a more complete analysis tool for architects and designers.

C4 STUDIO®. Modeled with Form•Z, rendered with StudioPro

It's Not Just CADD Anymore

ver the past decade computer aided design drafting (CADD) has been the method used to accomplish the construction document phase of a project on personal computers. Because of the labor-intensive nature of producing working drawings, the design profession was eager to automate this element of its practice. CADD promised to be the catalyst to revolutionize the practice of design, and so designers from all disciplines flocked to computer stores to purchase this tool that was intended to replace the drafting board. CADD applications and computers were so new to these designers that they concentrated the majority of their efforts on making the system work. Even the small to medium-sized firms hired "system managers" who, because of their training, still did not have a clear understanding of how architecture and related design practices functioned. There was enough research material that pointed out that computers would be a very productive drafting tool. However, design firms refused to investigate whether the computer could have been used for other tasks within the office. Consequently, the computer became and still continues to be only a CADD tool in many design practices. This does not make sense, since drafting, although extremely important, represents only a small portion of the activities that take place within a design practice.

A TALE OF TWO INDUSTRY LEADERS

Almost ten years after CADD applications began to appear on the VAX and UNIX platforms, Autodesk introduced AutoCAD to the masses using the personal computer in the early eighties. AutoCAD was an instant hit with design firms for now they had an opportunity to automate their production drawings and be more competitive with the larger firms. AutoCAD infiltrated the universities and established itself as the standard application for CADD within the design community. However, a decade after its introduction, AutoCAD is still a drafting production tool that has been dependent on technological advances made to personal computers and Intel processors.

When one thinks about the changing nature of the design profession and how diversified we have to be as designers, it is amazing to accept that Autodesk has not continued to develop. There have been upgrades to this application; however, these have only included minor fixes and additional features that do not take the next step from drafting to true design productivity. Instead of developing AutoCAD as a total integrated application, Autodesk has chosen to create a series of complementary products meant to be used in conjunction with AutoCAD. The problem with this is that along with AutoCAD, design firms must still purchase additional applications for creating solid computer-generated models, photorealistic renderings, animation, and NURBS surfacing modeling designs.

In the early seventies, Intergraph Corporation introduced a product called IGDS on the UNIX platform. Due to the enormous cost associated with the purchase of a UNIX system at the time, only the very large design firms were able to afford to incorporate this CADD application into their practices. IGDS was advanced for its time. It not only included sophisticated tools to relieve the burden of producing manual production drawings but also incorporated advanced visualization tools for creating computer-generated models. At that time Intergraph's CAD application only ran on the UNIX platform meaning that although small to medium-sized firms were teased by the potential of this technology, they were locked out.

Four years ago Intergraph decided to port its IGDS CAD application to the personal computer and began selling this product under the name MicroStation. This was a milestone for the design community; it meant that almost 20 years of development on the VAX and UNIX platform was about to be ported to the personal computer. Because of this evolution, MicroStation has a lot of "big system capabilities," such as networking (being able to share information in real time among all the members of the design team), distributive databases, and supporting concurrent designers and consultants through reference files. Due to its 20-year history and development, all of these and other functions in MicroStation are very mature.

MicroStation on the PC and Macintosh is a fully integrated design application that includes the most powerful production drafting tools on the market. In addition, this application is equipped with visualization tools to create computer-generated models, photorealistic renderings, animation, and NURBS surface modeling designs. This application is an office productivity tool that truly extends the way designers work.

THE DIRECTION OF THE MARKET

Many of the major CADD developers have now recognized the deficiencies in their CAD products and are moving aggressively to produce a CAD package that reflects an integrated approach to solving design problems. In order to be competitive, small and medium-sized firms must break away from the traditional CADD tool that focuses solely on drafting and incorporate into their practices an application that addresses all of their needs in a manner that is easy to use and is an extension of the way design is practiced. In this ever increasing marketplace you must have the best integrated design tools in order to increase your market share and be more competitive.

TOOLS TO LOOK FOR WHEN CHOOSING THE IDEAL CAD APPLICATION

Even though computers have been a part of the practice of design for the last decade, there are many in the design community for whom computers and their software applications are still very intimidating. In many design firms, project designers, project architects, project managers and principals have all stayed away from computer design tools. As a result, a subculture of CADD technicians and temporary CADD agencies has been created. This method of practice must change, and everyone in a design practice must take full advantage of the computer and its complementary CAD tools.

AN INVITING GRAPHICAL USER INTERFACE

For many years, designers have stayed away from DOS-based computers because of the many commands that have to be remembered in order to even get into the software application. After getting into the application, there are still more DOS-based commands to remember. The fact is that designers are not computer programmers and have no desire to be such. As designers, we just want to have access to automated tools that can increase our productivity throughout the design of a project. For this reason Apple's Macintosh has been the computer of choice for many designers. Its graphical user interface (GUI) is intuitive, easy to use, and extremely user friendly. As a result, designers who purchase Apple's Macintosh or Quadra computers can be productive right out of the box.

The response and accolades that Apple received for making a computer that is easy to use did not go unnoticed by the IBM-compatible personal computing industry. When Intergraph introduced MicroStation to the PC, the software application was outfitted with a new GUI based on OSF/Motif standards. The feel and appearance of this GUI is very consistent with Microsoft's Windows standard. MicroStation's motif GUI with pull-down menus, tool pallets, and dialog boxes presents designers with an environment in which they can feel much more comfortable to experiment, interact, and be productive with a powerful CAD program. The excitement that Apple Computers generated with its GUI is now being echoed throughout the IBM compatible computer industry, because of the similar user-friendly GUI of Microsoft's Windows. Consequently, traditional DOS and Macintosh-based applications such as AutoCAD and ArchiCAD are now being developed for the Microsoft's Windows GUI.

CUSTOMIZE YOUR WORKING ENVIRONMENT

One of the many reasons that designers still hold onto the traditional ways in which design was practiced is because they had control over all the tools. They could adjust a parallel bar or T-square; adjust the angles of an adjustable triangle; use an architectural scale to design and lay out physical spaces; use an engineering scale for site design; and most importantly have the tools on their desks that related to the job at hand. This is the kind of design practice flexibility that has not been integrated into CAD software applications until recently.

With a high-end application like Intergraph's
MicroStation, designers now have the capacity to change the
look and feel of the GUI between Motif and Microsoft's
Windows interface. This means that designers can choose the
environment that they are most comfortable and, consequently,
most productive in. This is a choice that did not exist when all
CAD applications were developed for DOS. If your experience
using computers has been with Apple's computers, then you
will feel very much at home, since both Motif and Windows
GUIs are very similar to Apple's. The key is to choose the
working environment that yields maximum production.

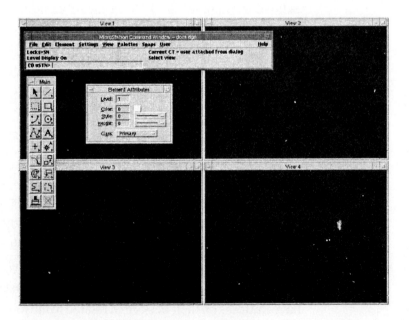

MicroStation's Motif Graphical User Interface

... designers now have the capacity to change the look and feel of the graphical user interface between Motif and Microsoft's popular Windows interface.

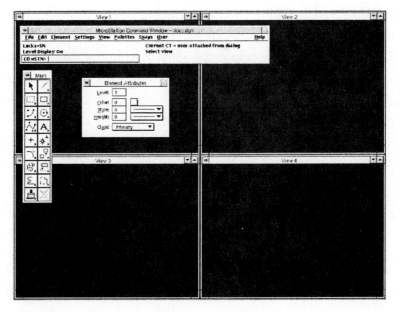

MicroStation's Windows Graphical User Interface

CUSTOMIZE YOUR WORKSPACE TO BE
CONSISTENT WITH THE WAY YOU DESIGN

Once you have chosen which of the environments such as Motif or Windows to work in, the next step toward efficiency and productivity is to customize your workspace. In the context of this discussion, a workspace is a customized environment for specific types of design offices and for users at different levels of experience. If, for example, an application is sold with approximately 100 tools, this does not mean that you have to use each of these tools if your type of design practice does not require them. Remember, CAD applications are only useful if they offer you the same degree of flexibility with its tools as you have with traditional tools such as T-squares, triangles, erasers, tracing paper, and pens and pencils. As a result, the ideal CAD application must give you the flexibility to customize your workspace. For example, if your practice is solely drafting, interior design, urban planning, landscape design, mapping, or facility management, MicroStation gives you the ability to select the tools that are consistent with these design disciplines. Even if you have been an ardent AutoCAD user and have decided to switch to MicroStation, you have the choice to select a workspace that has the look and feel of AutoCAD's workspace.

The objective here is to be able to select specialized tools for unique repetitive tasks and to hide or delete the tools that are not needed. Since designers do not have to search every pull-down menu, drawing tool, or dialog box for the appropriate tool, productivity increases.

When you purchase a CAD application, there is no reason for you or your designers to take months to be productive. After all, once you have been trained in your discipline, you can be immediately productive if you choose to use traditional design tools. Consequently, the CAD application you purchase must give you the flexibility to perform your duties within a workspace that is compatible with your experience. In a design practice, productivity means finishing the project on time; therefore, every effort should be made to shorten the learning curve of these applications by providing a workspace for new users, intermediate users, and advanced users.

Having access to workspaces that are consistent with the manner in which you practice design and appropriate to your level or experience gives new and experienced designers alike the opportunity to be productive with sophisticated applications like MicroStation, "right out of the box." In addition to workspaces, it is imperative that CAD applications be equipped with on-line help, especially for new users. Even advanced users may run into a function that is new, and who has the time to flip through the bundle of manuals ? On-line help is literally at your fingertips, to explain most of the functions and tools included in a CAD application.

New user workspace can be customized to be compatible with the level of user skill. In so doing users can be productive with the CAD application "right out of the box."

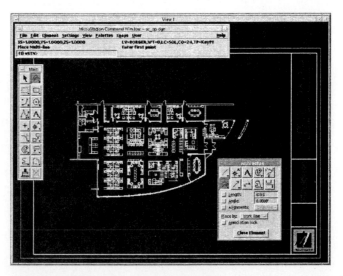

This is an example of a customized workspace for the practice of architecture. As you can see in the bottom right floating palette, all the frequently used architecture design tools are readily accessible.

Since the design workforce is so diversified in training and experience, workspaces can be an indispensable tool for principals, project managers, and project architects to achieve consistency and quality assurance. In this way, company standards are established and the flow of design information is uniform and clear to all of the design team.

A FEW INDISPENSABLE DESIGN TOOLS
Custom Line Styles

I have bittersweet memories of my days as an intern, creating wall details and then painfully delineating the section with attributes such as batt insulation. In addition, I learned that the true significance of an Exacto knife was for more than building models. There is a certain precise skill that an intern has to acquire in order to slice pieces of Zip-a-Tone to be pasted on the plans and elevations of each design. However, the developers of the new wave of CAD applications have heard the cries of interns and designers alike and have responded with simple tools for these time-consuming tasks. They can now be accomplished with a stroke of the mouse. These custom lines can be given attributes such as name, dash and gap pattern, width, offset, point symbol, and scale, and can even be saved in a library for use in other projects. These lines not only represent batt insulation but also a variety of custom lines like boundary lines, plumbing, section cuts, and fire-rated walls used regularly in architectural drawings.

Automating the task significantly increases productivity.

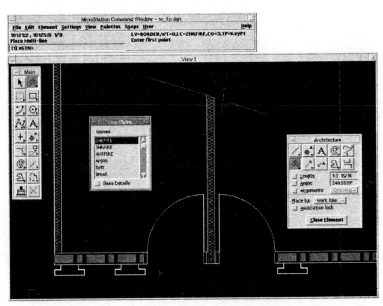

With the custom line tool batt insulation can be drawn as a line.

<u>Associative Hatching and Patterning</u>

In design there is always a need to distinguish one space from another, to differentiate private from public spaces; circulation path; loft space from core spaces; and waiting areas from serving areas. These differentiations are normally made with hatched or patterned lines. Both traditional drafting and previous CADD applications have made this process very tedious. With MicroStation, this design delineation can now be performed by entering a single data point anywhere within the desired area, which is then flooded with a hatching pattern.

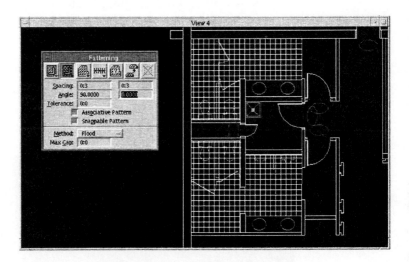

Flood fill cross-hatching can be used to illustrate spaces such as circulation paths and private and public areas.

Generating Site Profiles

As a designer, it is certain that at some time you have encountered a very challenging site that had to be cut, filled or manipulated in some manner in order to accommodate the building or a landform. The proper design of such sites cannot be efficiently studied using cardboard models or "guess-timates." It is sophisticated tools like the section tool in MicroStation that designers need to continue to be competitive.

This design tool, which was previously only available in expensive civil engineering applications, is used to generate a section cut through a model to illustrate interior soil detail for design decision making. This tool can speed up the generation of section geometry for complex sites and any potential problems that relate to the placement of a structure can be addressed very early in the design process.

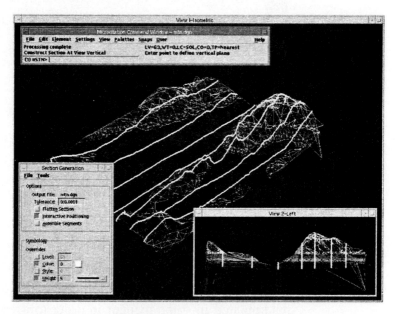

... visualize and analyze profiles of the proposed site of your project with the Section Generator tool.

DESIGN VISUALIZATION

As noted earlier in this chapter, any CAD application that is serious about increasing productivity must include visualization tools for 3D model construction, texture mapping capabilities for assigning materials onto the model for rendering, and animation functionality for design analysis. In order for the application to be truly integrated, these tools must be part of the software, and not purchased as separate applications.

The rendering capability of Intergraph's MicroStation is quite impressive when compared to other specialized rendering software applications.

ON-LINE DESIGN REVIEW FROM YOUR DESK

For all designers, building and zoning code compliance, quality assurance, and abiding by the rules of local and municipal boards are concerns that must be addressed throughout the design of a project. In the traditional practice, major reviews of the design occur at the end of each design phase. In this case, drawings are plotted and distributed to each member of the design team, the client, and members of these boards who have an interest in the proposed design. This process is wasteful and time consuming, at least for members of the design team. In the office, design reviews can be conducted directly from the desks of members of the design team. The ability to review design solutions in-house as well as with consultants at a remote site, all on line, would provide members of the team with tools to view, redline, and discuss alternative design solutions – simultaneously and interactively across a local area network (LAN). It is important to note that these changes, notes, and redlines would be automatically stored in a reference file and would not affect the integrity of the original design drawings.

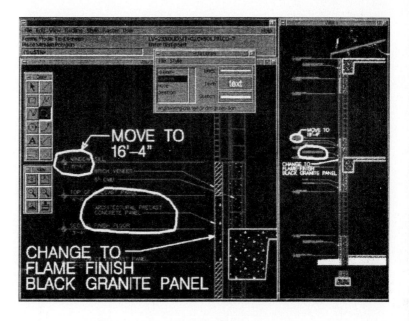

Using MicroStation Review, designers can electronically make appropriate changes while conducting remote meetings with associates, consultants or client.

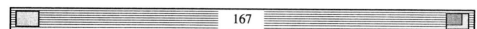

167

C4 STUDIO©, Modeled with Form•Z, rendered with StudioPro

DESIGN COMMUNICATION
AND THE
ELECTRONIC AGORA

ood communication among all members of a design team has always been a prerequisite for producing functional design. With the fall of the Berlin Wall, Glasnost, the end of apartheid in South Africa, and the lifting of cultural and economic barriers by Asian nations like Japan, design firms of all sizes have begun to jump at the opportunities to practice in these nations, mainly through joint ventures with native design firms. As an employee at RTKL Associates in 1986, I remember beginning to do business in Japan. Today RTKL Associates is a prominent foreign design firm involved with major commissions in Japan. Small to medium-sized firms have witnessed the success of large firms like RTKL Associates and are beginning to join forces with other firms with complementary skills and abilities in order to be more competitive. What these large firms have done is not new; throughout history, designers have always adapted their practices to political and economic changes.

The political developments described above, have begun to affect the practice of design. Consequently, design firms must effectively manage the flow of information throughout their practices as well as to key principals such as clients, consultants, contractors, building and zoning code officials, and financiers.

Throughout the life of a project, these participants are involved in such activities as accounting, marketing, project proposals, business development, contracts, project scheduling, project management, financial feasibility analysis, construction cost estimating, life-cycle costing, fee proposals, operating expenses, payroll, correspondence, meeting planning, transmittals and building program analysis, agreements, contract documents, design submissions and approval, change orders, submission of bidding documents, transmittals, legal matters, and insurance. The need for good communication among these functions is clear.

THE ELECTRONIC AGORA

In ancient Greece, the agora stood at the center of cities and it was their communication heart. It was the place where communication of vital importance happened. Politicians, philosophers, intellectuals, the religious, the wealthy, the powerful, all came to the agora to communicate their ideas to their constituents. From this central location information was then, dissipated throughout the city. Through this social ritual everyone was kept informed of current and future plans. The agora served as a " feeding ground" for good communication. The need for good communication that manifested itself at the agora in ancient Greece is now the challenge and the opportunity facing the design community ... "The Electronic Agora."

DESIGN COMMUNICATION SOLUTIONS

Rapid developments in the computer software, hardware, and fiber-optic industries have contributed to making the computer an electronic agora. These developments are represented in local area networks (LAN), electronic mail (E-mail), on-line computer services, and computer video conferencing. The common dominator in each of these systems if the fact that information is communicated, and then dissipated. Computers bring the agora to your design office, via your desktop computer and a modem. This electronic agora gives designers the power to communicate with anyone in this new global marketplace, retrieve valuable information, dissipate marketing materials, electronically submit bids for projects throughout the world, communicate with joint-venture partners on different continents, and, probably most importantly, work on design projects with different remote design partners and consultants simultaneously.

COMMUNICATION VIA LOCAL AREA NETWORKS (LAN)

Before we get into the benefits of incorporating a LAN system into your design practice, it is important to briefly discuss the origin of this technology. There is no doubt that the flow of information would be better communicated among all parties on the design team if their computers were networked. This was the premise adopted by the early developers of LAN systems.

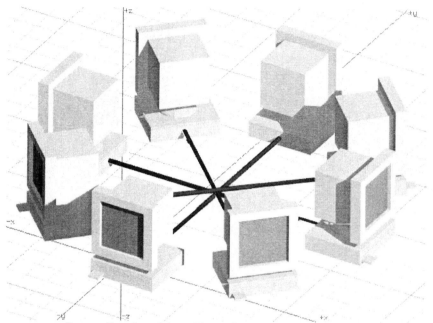

Peer-to-Peer Local Area Network (LAN) system.

However, when LAN technology was initially introduced to the design community, it was presented as *"client-server networks,"* to meet the needs of the few large design firms with extensive budgets.

Client server networks comprise one or more dedicated " servers " which serve the " clients" of the network. Instead of using the computers already in place in your office to build a network system, you have to purchase additional computers, to act as servers, and to handle the tasks of storing and distributing files and data to each member of the design team connected to the network. Throughout firms, these servers control all electronic data and activities such as file access, printing, plotting, networking, and security.

Whether your practice is large or medium-sized, all documents related to a project are channeled through and accessed from these centrally located, expensive client servers. This technology may work well for large corporations, but it was not designed to accommodate the practice of design. Large design firms spent considerable sums of money and hired system managers to make client server networks conform to their design practices.

Designers have worked in and perpetuated the team concept as the best approach for executing a design project. The team concept lends itself to a communication system in which everyone on the team has micro control of all data that relates to the design project. Instead of having design teams in your firm access files and peripherals from one central client server, why not have design nodes in which each design team can function independently? This is a much more productive way to work. It is also easier to manage and less vulnerable to a system crash. Why have the entire office staff dependent on this central server unproductive for the period during which the system manager attempts to fix the problem? If a design firm implements a system in which each design team uses an alternative network system that is independent of a central server, then the possibility of each network system being down at the same time will be lessened. As designers we must look for and use tools that more closely conform to the practice of design.

Client server networking may serve the purposes of corporate America and a few large design firms, but it certainly is not representative of team design, nor does this technology serve the needs of the majority of design firms that are small to medium in size.

Unlike client server networks that have been designed to serve the needs of a few large design firms, *"peer-to-peer network systems"* focus on the needs of the many small to medium-sized design firms that constitute the bulk of the market. This technology also conforms to the team concept of design. Peer-to peer network systems like Artisoft's LANtastic allow design firms to network their existing PCs instead of having to incur the additional expense of purchasing high-powered computers to act as dedicated servers. If you have a small design practice and have not upgraded your computers for the last few years, you can add your older DOS-based XTs or MAC-based SEs to a peer-to-peer network. In addition, the flexibility of this technology allows each computer on the network to function as servers, clients, or both. This gives everyone on the design team access to all design data, software applications, and peripherals attached to the network. As a result, the project manager can read a file from the project architect's computer or plot a file from the CADD technician's computer.

Advantages of using Peer-to-Peer Networking

Peer-to-peer networking, is easily integrated into the practice of design and fosters good communication among the design team. In addition, the low startup cost, ease of use, and low support and maintenance costs make peer-to-peer networking affordable. On your network, designers and support staff will have the opportunity to access peripherals such as laser and color printers, CD-ROMs, scanners, plotters, and storage and backup drives.

NO NETWORK SYSTEM IS AN ISLAND

As the cost of personal computers decreases, the design community has been purchasing computers for specific tasks. For example, since Aldus Corporation introduced PageMaker – the software that defined desktop publishing— for Apple's Macintosh platform, design firms have discovered that they not only have greater control over all marketing material that can be targeted to specific clients, but can also save significant cost. As a result, Artisoft LANtastic and a few other DOS-based peer-to-peer networks would give your firm the capability to connect and add a *LocalTalk* network of Apple computers. This means that users of a DOS-based or Macintosh-based network can share laser and color printers, scanners and plotters, and access files on storage and backup drives that reside on either network through a dedicated PC that functions as a communication gateway.

This development in peer-to-peer networking is extremely important to the design community, who have depended on office productivity software applications originally developed for the Macintosh platform. Since the advent of Microsoft's Windows GUI, many Apple developers have begun to port their applications to IBM compatible computers to operate under Windows. This is good news because these software developers are producing seamless and parallel applications for both the Macintosh and Window GUI's. For example, products such as Intergraph's MicroStation, Microsoft Excel, Microsoft Word, Claris's FileMaker Pro, Aldus's PageMaker, and Adobe's PhotoShop are the exact applications running under Apple's Macintosh and Quadras, and Microsoft's Windows interfaces. As a result, files created in any such application can be accessed by users of either network without translation. In addition, since the applications are identical on the Macintosh and Windows platforms, no new training is required.

SECURITY

One of the most important elements in peer-to-peer networking is security. Within a design team there is certain information that needs to be confidential . For example, there is no need for a CADD technician to know what the budget for a project is, nor how changes in the design are affecting this budget. This type of information should be controlled by the project manager. Consequently, special access accounts need to be set up for each member of the design team to give them restrictive access to designated servers and peripherals.

Implementation of such a security system can be configured to include user name and password. In addition the security system can be further designed to give users the privilege to delete, read, modify files, or search for research-specific design data located on the server. Some peer-to-peer networks like Artisoft LANtastic go a step further and assign passwords to peripherals, track log-ins and log-outs, track account expiration dates, restrict user times and privileges, and track unauthorized attempts to enter locked files. In essence, everyone on the design team has the ability to decide and manage his or her own localized network.

COMMUNICATIONS – MODEM

How much time is spent by you and your employees traveling to and from project meetings and professional development seminars or in and out of airports? How much of your profit is spent on plane tickets, hotel rooms, meals, and so on? Do you think you would be more productive if you could spend some of that time in the office doing other work?

If the answer to these questions is yes, then, courtesy of your computer and communications applications, you could be doing just that.

We do business with clients all over this country and collaborate with associates internationally, conducting several conferences over the modem using software applications like Farallon's Timbuktu Pro. With this application you can transfer files smoothly between Mac and Windows users. Now we know how many unnecessary meetings are held during the design and construction phase of a project. In addition, it never seems possible to stay on course with the intended agenda. Someone always goes off on a tangent, and although you may be billing the client for time spent in this meeting, it sometimes seems a waste when you consider that this time could have been better spent finding new projects or completing another project. After a meeting, the participants go back to their respective offices, mull over notes from the meeting, and play telephone tag trying to reach consultants or the client in order to clarify issues discussed in the meeting. *Then another meeting is held to discuss potential findings. There has to be an alternative approach to the business of design.*

Using Farallon's Timbuktu Pro and modems hooked up to your computers, you have the ability to host meetings right from your office with every member of your design team, the consultants and the owner. This approach allows everyone to see each other's monitor screen, access each other's files, present options, work interactively, and make swift and accurate decisions in real time. Like a traditional telephone conference, a Timbuktu remote session allows any participant to become the host and share his or her screen with all other participants.

Participants can share graphics, texts, design solutions, 3D computer models, renderings, animations, CADD documents, specifications, change orders, shop drawings, and meeting minutes. All this can be accomplished without leaving your office. The cost ? A telephone call. Savings? No impromptu lunches or dinners after the meeting. No time wasted traveling back and forth to the meeting site. No time lost in airports waiting for your flight or traveling in the friendly skies. Once you arrive in the designated city, no time spent traveling to and from the airport. How much time and money do you think can be saved by all parties ?

Imagine doing this for your next client meeting. You can hook up to your client's computer and make your presentation without ever leaving the office. Your client can view the presentation, approve or disapprove, suggest changes or not, all over the telephone. What other tasks in your office could benefit from applying the same concept ?

ELECTRONIC CHARETTE / COLLABORATIVE REMOTE DESIGNING

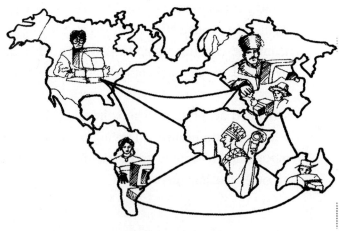

Can you imagine several designers, at different locations, working on the same design problem at the same time? Each designer able to see the other's screen, operate each other's machine, suggest and make changes to the project and, actually complete a project, all across telephone lines?

This is being done and you can do it too. Farallon's Timbuktu Pro could help you open doors to new ways of doing business globally. These are features that were unavailable to small to medium-sized firms just a few years ago. Remote design collaboration would allow your firm to enter into joint ventures with other designers throughout the country and internationally. For example, if your firm has just won the bid for a design project in the Middle East, there is no need for you to set up shop in that region or have a working knowledge of their customs. Use the resources of a native designer who lives there and has first-hand knowledge of the cultural customs. Instead of conducting your weekly design meetings in the Middle East, conduct these meetings from the comfort of your office. As a small to medium-sized firm you must change the mindset and cultural thinking of your practice and think how you can continue to be competitive and how computers can be fully integrated into your practice to make it more productive.

Many government agencies and high-tech clients have already begun to accept electronic submissions in response to requests for proposals (RFPs). In the nineties, instead of spending and "don't leave home without it," your motto should be " why leave home at all?"

COMMUNICATION VIA ELECTRONIC MAIL (E-MAIL)

Electronic mail refers to messages that are transmitted from computer to computer over ordinary telephone lines under the direction of an intermediate service like AIA *Online*. This service is a "host" computer that receives messages, holds them, and sends them to the proper destination. With this system, it is not necessary for the sender and receiver of a message to be connected simultaneously. A user of E-mail needs a computer, a modem, a printer, a telephone line, and an E-mail service. Electronic voice mail operates in a similar fashion, electronically storing voice messages. Electronic mail applications like cc:Mail work on both Apple's Macintosh and IBM compatible computers over a LAN or standalone computers.

"How many times have you received an important message on your voice mail that is difficult to understand. If you even understand the caller's name and telephone number you have to call him/her back for clarification. The person is out of his or her office, and you have to either leave a message with the secretary or leave a voice mail message which may or may not be clear. For whatever reason your call is returned two days later."

Send your associate an Electronic Mail message!

INCREASE YOUR FIRM'S PRODUCTIVITY WITH ONLINE SERVICES

You may have heard of or participated in computer sessions hosted by online services such as CompuServe, America Online, or Internet. These services conduct several forums for the architecture and design profession, as well as give in-depth information on almost every aspect of the computer industry. However, as illustrated throughout this book, designers need targeted solutions that address the specific needs of their profession. Although important as an information resource, none of the online services mentioned above specifically targets or addresses the needs of the design community. This is where the American Institute of Architects on-line (AIA Online) service comes in.

The AIAOnline computer service provides vital information and communication services to architects, interior designers, urban planners, landscape designers, engineers, product manufacturers, specifiers, and information vendors working in the building industry. This service is accessible through the use of a modem-equipped computer and a local telephone call. To address the needs of designers at any time, the service is available 24 hours a day, 365 days a year.

AIAOnline provides your firm with :

Access to industry publications such as R.S. Means, Architecture, Interiors, portions of Masterspec, and government guide specifications. You can also access the AIA Library and Archives catalog, as well as AIAOnline's electronic bookstore to order reports, publications, and products, 24 hours a day, 365 days a year.

Find vital business leads that would give you the strategic edge in your practice found in:
$ Commerce Business Daily
$ State procurement notices
$ Reuter
$ World Bank notices
$ PR Newswire
$ Commercial construction
$ Federal news services
$ Industry press releases

Connect to resource networks through numerous electronic forums covering such topics as health care facilities, housing, interiors, and urban and regional development. Each forum includes meeting notices and newsletters. In addition, your firm would have access to the employment referral bulletin board, which can assist you in filling positions vacancies.

Locate important business and professional contacts in a matter of seconds.

Need a firm for a joint venture project that complements your type of practice and specializes in the type of design for the proposed project? AIAOnline gives you immediate access to :

§ Architects
§ Contractors
§ Engineers
§ Product manufacturers with online CADD drawing of their products
§ Consulting firms
§ Interior design, urban planning, and landscape design firms

Electronic mail service is available so you can send and receive company communications or mail from project administrators, and product manufacturers' representatives, transmit CAD/project files, and conduct professional and business networking.

Other miscellaneous services such as Architectural Registration Board information, professional development and event calendars, specifications, codes and standards, costing information, and insurance and related services are all a telephone call away, 24 hours a day, 365 days a year.

... All The Design Communication Tools You Need To Increase Productivity Without Increasing Staff, And Yet Remain Competitive!

C4 STUDIO0, Modeled with Form-Z, rendered with StudioPro

ACCOUNTING

FOR

DESIGN

our accounting practices and procedures can make or break your business. Assuming that you have some bookkeeping system in place now, let us talk about automating that system to give you a better handle on your business. There are many products available that can meet the specific needs of your business. As with other applications, however, the usefulness, or the lack thereof, will depend mostly on whether you can choose the right product for your business.

Along with hardware considerations, you have to match the features of the package with the needs of your business. As far as hardware requirements go, check for memory and hard disk recommendations on the package, and refer to the chapter on hardware for further clarification if needed.

Le us talk about the features. Initially, your choice is between integrated and modular programs.

Integrated - all the functions come in one package
Modular - each function is purchased separately.

In general, integrated packages cost less but also offer fewer features. In this case, *less is not more!* Modular packages will generally offer more features for their higher price tag, but the advantage is that you have the option of only purchasing those modules that you need.

You should discuss your needs with your accountant before you buy. He or she may already be using a package and can help you make the best decision for your business, and even help with the transition. While these packages will not eliminate the need for an accountant, they will help you get a better financial picture of your business. Armed with this information, you can make confident and profitable decisions. Larger firms should consult with their financial controller. Changing over to an automated system has many benefits, but it does require someone with the financial knowledge to correctly set up account charts and other financial data.

Among the integrated packages, there are some that are set up specifically for service-type businesses like ours. While such packages do not address every need, the help they offer in managing time and clients is very useful. You can track the time each employee spends with each client.

```
┌─────────────────────────────────────────────────────────┐
│ ▦▦▦▦▦▦▦▦▦▦▦▦▦▦▦▦▦ TSTimerApp ▦▦▦▦▦▦▦▦▦▦▦▦▦▦▦▦▦ │
│ Slip 9      of 42        inactive           0  active slips ┌─────────┐│
│                                    Slip Value $ 0.00        │Mini View││
│ ◄ ▓▓▓▓▓▓         ▷                                          └─────────┘│
│  ┌──────────┐                                ● 0.00      ┌─────────┐│
│  │   User   │ CBC Curtis B                              │ Turn on ││
│  ├──────────┤ Presentation                   ○ 0.00     └─────────┘│
│  │ Activity │                                           ·············│
│  ├──────────┤ Northeast                      ○ 0.00     ┌─────────┐│
│  │  Client  │                                           │ Delete  ││
│  └──────────┘                                ○ Fixed value └───────┘│
│                                                          ┌─────────┐│
│ Showed rough ideas of new pitch to Mr. ⬆  ○ Billable     │ Revert  ││
│ Roberts; he enjoyed them and gave Bill the  ● Unbillable └─────────┘│
│ contract                                    ○ No Charge  ┌─────────┐│
│                                             ○ Hold       │  Help   ││
│                                          ⬇  ○ Summary    └─────────┘│
│                                                          Found: 0   │
│  Date │3/5/90│            Time Estimated │0:45:00│               ⬆  │
│  thru │3/5/90│  ┌──────┐       Spent     │0:20:31│ ▦              │
│                 │ Time │                                         ⬇  │
│  ☐ Recurring              ☐ Add to Flat Fee                        │
└─────────────────────────────────────────────────────────┘
```

"Slip" from Timeslip.

Initially, you input your employees and their rates
(multiple rate levels available); your tasks, and any rates
associated with them; and your clients and their rates. Then
you create a "slip" with information that includes the employee
name, client name, project description, billing rate, time
budgeted and time actually spent. You have the option to
charge based on a client rate, an employee (user) rate, or a task
(activity) rate. Included on the slip is a timer. You indicate the
time spent on the particular task (or you can actually start the
timer when you begin your encounter – telephone call, meeting,
or other task – and when you're finished, you stop the timer)
so, if you charge an hourly rate for your particular service, all
the information is calculated from the slip.

Using this information, you can:

1. Bill your clients more accurately.
2. Generate reports to :
   - evaluate employee productivity
   - evaluate client's activity
   - track and age accounts receivable
   - track the progress of a project and all the
     financial information that goes with it.

Information about your clients includes everything from name and address (for billing purposes and mailing labels) to interest, markups, and applicable taxes, to client's budget and funds held in escrow for the client.

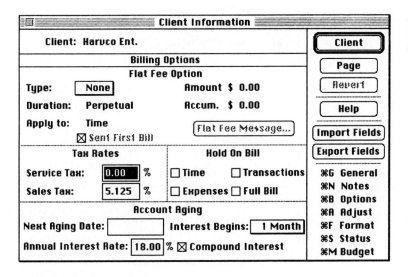

Timeslip's billing options

Timeslip's billing format screen

Timeslip's billing status screen

Specialized software designed specifically for architects and engineers for use in the construction industry is another option, albeit a more expensive one. These programs address all the accounting needs of the firm, its clients and its projects. Typically they are divided into modules so that you can purchase only what you need.

In addition to the features already listed, accounts payable and payroll are available. Many different billing methods unique to architectural, engineering, and construction firms are allowed – for example, "phased fixed fee" and "phased percent of construction costs."

Advantages include :

1.) integration with various project management
   applications for a complete accounting solution.
2.) distribute your accounts payable costs among
   many projects.
3.) transfer time sheet data from the project, thereby
   automating payroll.
4.) produce invoices specific to the field, e.g., change
   order invoices

Other useful features of an automated accounting system include its ability to produce custom invoices, reports, and financial statements so that you will have a clear financial picture of your business at any given time. You can customize bills to meet both your and your client's needs. You decide how much (or how little) detail will appear on the bill, such as:

Consultant's fees   Fixed fees
Percent of total fee   Fee by phase
Dates   Overdue notices
Direct personal expenses
(for government contracts)

From the time and expense information you put into your computer, you can get back very useful reports that can help you run your business more efficiently and more profitably. Most applications also give you the added option of entering a budget so that you can see where you stand with respect to budgeted costs versus actual costs. Reports include:

Time reports and analyses by project, employee, and client
Nonbillable hours and estimated lost earnings
Client activity reports
Current project-to-date costs and budget

Use the reports to evaluate and improve your use of time and resources in your business and much more.

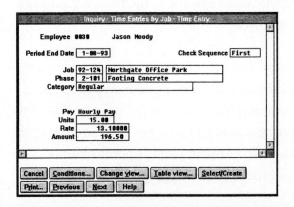

With Timberline Gold AEC software you can track the time that each employee spends on specific parts of a project, in order to better manage the overall budget of the project.

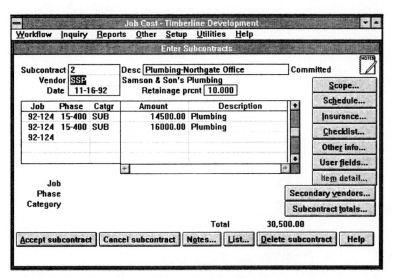

Timberline's architecture and engineering specific software offers the opportunity to track and manage details such as the subcontractor's costs associated with a project . Additional information like the scope and schedule for this phase of the project can also be accessed from within the same screen.

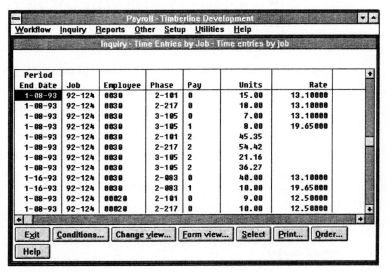

Track and correlate employee time to job numbers and even specific phases within the same job from the Payroll module

Account	Accountng Date	Transaction Desc	Debit	Credit
1032	11-16-92	HVAC Work	12,360.00	
1032	11-16-92	HVAC Work	7,500.00	
1032	11-16-92	Electrical	3,400.00	
1032	11-16-92	Plumbing	7,200.00	
1032	11-16-92	Plumbing	13,050.39	
1035	11-16-92	Studs 2 x 4	750.00	
1035	11-16-92	Sheetrock	700.00	
1035	11-16-92	Anderson Windows	1,250.00	
1035	11-16-92	Prehung Doors	800.00	
1035	11-16-92	Carpet	1,800.00	
2010	11-16-92	AP Enter manual check	1,500.00	
2010	11-16-92	AP Enter invoices sum		45,275.06-

General Ledger - Timberline Development

Workflow Inquiry Reports Other Setup Utilities Help

Inquiry - Transaction - Transaction Info

Exit   Conditions...   Notes...   Change view...   Form view...   Select   Print...
Order...   Help

Daily transaction information is at your fingertips

Other programs like M.Y.O.B. are pure accounting type programs applicable to most business types. They also allow you to set up accounts for clients and can furnish you with the same reports as the specialized programs. The difference is that you will have to do a little more work to customize the charts so that they conform to the needs of a design firm. They may or may not offer a payroll option. The interface may be different but the accounting principles are the same.

The bottom line is to check the list of features and match them to your business's requirements and your budget. More features do not necessarily make it a better program. What is right for you is the application that most closely matches your need.

C4 STUDIO©, Modeled with Form•Z, rendered with StudioPro

USING INTEGRATED
APPLICATIONS
TO
INCREASE PRODUCTIVITY

ntegrated packages are modular in nature and contain less "feature-filled" and less expensive versions of typical office software like a word processor, spreadsheet, database, a draw or paint program, and a communications module. The integrated package offers the ability to move easily between modules, transferring data while maintaining a consistent interface throughout the package. Integrated software packages can be an invaluable tool for the smaller office that may not have the budget or the need for a dedicated, standalone, word processor, database, or spreadsheet program.

ClarisWorks

Even though the package is inexpensive, it offers the most often used elements of each of its modules in one convenient package. Each package handles the integration via a different mechanism and you will have to look around to find the package that best suits you and the type of documentation that you typically produce in your office.

We can, however, look at some of the general features that apply to most of these applications.

In the word processor, you can add headers and footers, footnotes, and multiple columns to give your documents a professional look. You also have features like mail merge that allow you to combine your letters with your database files to create personalized letters. Spell check your documents and access the thesaurus to correct and improve your writing.

As designers, we can appreciate the mini drawing package that allows us to create, rotate, and place graphics and text. Import your logo and create company stationery; files from your drafting package can be placed in your documents to clients. Access a variety of colors and patterns that will help your documents truly look like they come from the desk of a designer.

In your database, you can organize your data in the format that suits your needs. Use the data for mailing labels or customer lists; create reports; design forms; do calculations between related fields using formulas that you create.

The spreadsheet module allows you to track and manipulate your financial data, use formulas, analyze " what - if scenarios" and transform your data into charts. The charting feature is particularly interesting because it allows you to view your spreadsheet as either a pie chart, a bar chart, a line chart, or a scatter chart.

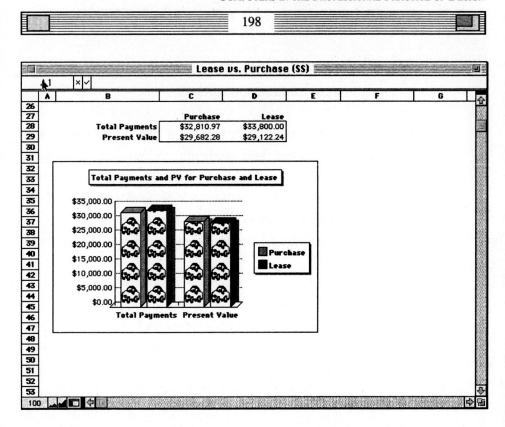

The charting feature automatically creates a chart using values from your spreadsheet.

After you have finished creating your document, you can use the communications module and your modem to send it to your client's desk or maybe to his or her mailbox on CompuServe. You can save your document in a variety of formats so that it can be understood by your client's word processor, which may not be the same as your own.

Let us look at one application's approach to integrating the modules discussed above. It uses a feature called "frames" allowing you to use the functions of each of the modules individually or in combination. Individually, you can work in either your word processor, spreadsheet, database, drawing, or communications environments. Using the frame technology, though, you can create a single, compound document combining several modular environments.

For instance, you can place a spreadsheet frame, a word processing frame, and a database frame all in the same document. You can establish a link between the frames so that you can make changes in one frame and have them automatically updated in any linked frames. When you click in the spreadsheet frame, the menu bar changes to reflect the spreadsheet commands. When you are finished making changes to the spreadsheet, you can click outside the spreadsheet box and move the box around like a graphic, placing it in any position in your document. Whichever frame is the active frame will have its menu bar displayed and it will be like you are working in that module. So, you have access to all the modules on a single page.

As I mentioned before, most of these "works" programs are scaled-back versions of standalone products. This is good news for you as your office grows. You may find that you need a full-blown database to accommodate your business activities, and it is nice to know that you can move up without having to learn a whole new program.

For example, Microsoft Works' word processor module is a sibling to Microsoft's premiere word processor, Word and ClarisWorks' database is sibling to Claris' popular database FileMaker Pro.

For added value, these programs ship with templates that many offices will find very useful. All the elements are already in place, all you have to do is customize them with your information to fit your specific needs. The templates include a newsletter, business card, resume and checkbook.

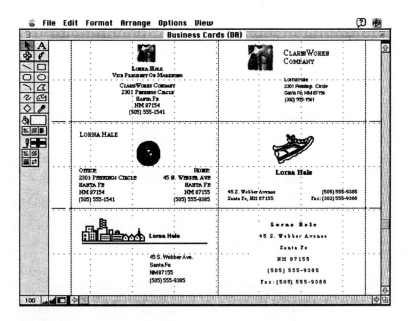

ClarisWorks provides you with business card templates that you can customize for your company.

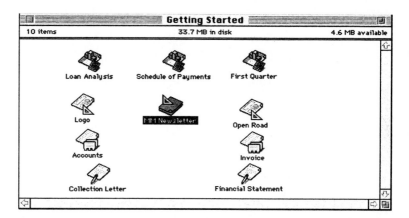

Small business templates shipped with Microsoft Works.

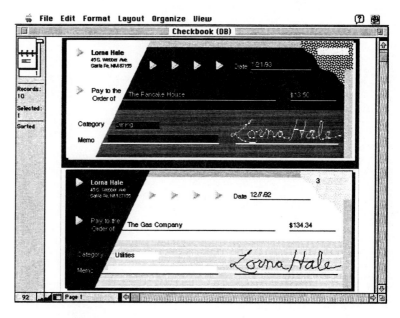

Checkbook template created in ClarisWorks database format allows
you to track your checking account.

As you can see, the " Works" programs really deliver the works! You really get more bang for the buck. For those of us whose office needs are fairly simple and routine, these programs are an excellent value.

C4 STUDIO©, Modeled with Form•Z, rendered with StudioPro

ERGONOMICS

rgonomics is defined as the applied science that coordinates the design of devices, systems, and physical working conditions with the capacities and requirements of the worker. To put it more simply, the science of comfort and convenience or fit and function. Applying ergonomic principles to your workplace can make you and your employees safer and more productive. It will help to reduce the incidence of injury and consequently decrease the number of sick days you or your employees will have to lose. It is important to remember that ergonomic considerations are not a luxury, they can actually save you money. Tests conducted by the National Institute of Occupational Safety and Health conclude that an ergonomically designed computer environment will increase operator productivity by as much as 24 percent !

Even before the advent of computers in the practice of design,designers should have been acutely aware of the ergonomic environment in which they worked. This is because designers tend to spend long hours at one task like drawing or drafting. The experts now recommend that you vary your tasks as much as possible. However, since that is not always possible, take at least a ten minute break for every hour spent doing repetitive tasks. (There are even computer programs that will remind you when it is time to take your break!)

It is important to keep ergonomics in mind when you purchase furniture for use in your office. Let us start with the chair. The chair you buy should have a variety of adjustments to facilitate changing positions and tasks. When you sit in your chair, your feet should be flat on the floor or you should purchase a footrest to keep your feet flat. You will also need adjustable armrests, back supports, and height and tilt adjustments to avoid problems such as back strain, irregular blood flow, and carpal tunnel syndrome. You can also purchase cushions or other devices to help alleviate back strain.

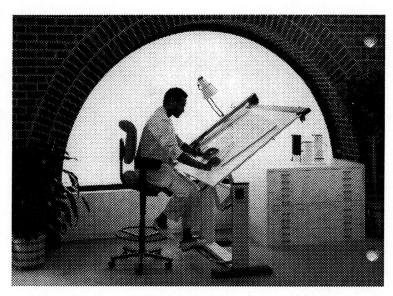

The Cyborg Chair from Rudd International

COMPUTER WORKSTATIONS

Work surfaces should also be adjustable. For the design profession, the key adjustments are height and the tilt of the desktop. For drawing, designers are accustomed to working on a tilted surface, and, there is no need to give that up because you work on a computer. It is still, ergonomically, better to draw on a tilted surface to protect neck and shoulder muscles. Keyboards stands should be positioned at the correct height, or support should be provided for the wrist so as not to injure the arm and shoulder muscles. Monitor stands should allow you to position your monitor about 20 degrees below your line of sight and, between 13 and 18 inches from your eyes. Monitor stands also free your desk, yielding more workspace.

Many of the features discussed can be purchased as a bundle in a workstation. The design station pictured here includes space for the CPU, monitor, keyboard, printers, and other peripherals, as well as a drawing surface. There are multiple versions of the workstation to accommodate your need and budget.

ERGOTRON Ergonomic Computer Workstation

Furniture should not be your only ergonomic consideration. Equipment you purchase should also be ergonomically designed as well. The devices that directly have an impact on the user are the mouse or stylus and the monitor. When purchasing a monitor, look for low-radiation screens to minimize your exposure to the radiation that can come from the screen. It is believed to be harmful although there is no conclusive medical evidence. Also, remember to purchase antiglare filters or purchase a monitor that has a screen with a special optical coating to make it glare resistant. It will cut down significantly on the eye strain.

The mouse or stylus used for drawing or drafting on the computer is undergoing several changes from the original version in an effort to make it more ergonomic. Mice come in a variety of shapes and sizes. In addition to offering more control for drawing and drafting, the stylus or pen-mouse also seems to offer a better ergonomic fit. Test one before purchsing.

The important thing to remember is adjustability. We are not all the same size and shape and it is important that our workspace be adjustable to each individual's varying needs and tasks.

C4 STUDIO©. Modeled with Form•Z, rendered with StudioPro

RESOURCE
GUIDE

3D STUDIO
AUTODESK
MODELING , ANIMATION AND
RENDERING

ACCESS PC
INSIGNIA
FILE CONVERSION

ACT!
CONTACT SOFTWARE
INTERNATIONAL
PERSONAL INFORMATION
MANAGER

ACURIS CLIP MODEL
LIBRARY
ACURIS
MODELING

ADOBE PREMIERE
ADOBE SYSTEMS INC.
POST ANIMATION EDITING

ALIAS SKETCH
ALIAS
PRODUCT DESIGN

ALIAS UPFRONT
ALIAS RESEARCH
CONCEPTUAL MODELING

ANIMATOR PRO
AUTODESK
ANIMATION

APERTURE
GRAPHIC MANAGEMENT
GROUP INC
FACILITY MANAGEMENT

ARCHICAD
GRAPHISOFT USA
CAD & VISUALIZATION

ARCHITRION II
UNIC AEC SOFTWARE
2D / 3D CAD

ASG MODEL VISION
ASG
2D / 3D CAD

AUTOCAD
AUTODESK
CAD

AUTOVISION
AUTODESK
RENDERING

BIG D
GRAPHICS SOFTWARE INC
RENDERING

BLOCKS & MATERIALS
KETIV & MODERN MEDIUM
MODELING & RENDERING

CADMOVER
KANDU SOFTWARE
CORPORATION
GRAPHIC TRANSLATION UTILITY

CC: MAIL
LOTUS DEVELOPMENT
CORPORATION
ELECTRONIC MAIL

CLARIS CAD
CLARIS CORPORATION
2D CAD

CLARIS RESOLVE
CLARIS CORPORATION
SPREADSHEET

CLARISWORKS
CLARIS CORPORATION
INTEGRATED SOFTWARE

COLOR STUDIO
LETRASET / FRACTAL DESIGN
IMAGE EDITING

CYBERSPACE DEVELOPMENT
KIT
AUTODESK
3D VISUALIZATION /
SIMULATION

DIGITAL DARKROOM
SILICONE BEACH SOFTWARE
IMAGE EDITING

DIVA VIDEO SHOP
DIVA CORPORATION
QUICK TIME ANIMATION /
PRESENTATION

ELASTIC REALITY
ELASTIC REALITY, INC.
PROFESSIONAL MORPHING

ELECTRIC IMAGE
ELECTRIC IMAGE ANIMATION
SYSTEM
ANIMATION & RENDERING

EXCEL
MICROSOFT
SPREADSHEET

EXTEND
IMAGINE THAT, INC.
SYSTEMS MODELING
PROGRAMMING

FAST TRACK SCHEDULE
AEC SOFTWARE
PROJECT SCHEDULING

FILEMAKER PRO
CLARIS CORPORATION
DATABASE

FONTMONGER
ARES SOFTWARE
CORPORATION
TYPE EDITOR

FORM•Z
AUTODESSYS
3D MODELING

FREEHAND
ALDUS CORPORATION
GRAPHIC DESIGN

GALLERY EFFECTS
ALDUS CORPORATION
IMAGE EDITING

GEOQUERY
GEOQUERY CORPORATION
LEAD TRACKING

GRAMMATIK
REFERENCE SOFTWARE
INTERNATIONAL
WRITING IMPROVEMENT

HYPERCARD DEVELOPER'S
KIT
CLARIS CORPORATION
PRESENTATION / AUTHORING

IMAGINE PUPPETEER
SCHREIBER INSTRUMENTS
PLUG-INS FOR ANIMATION

INFIN-D
SPECULAR INTERNATIONAL
*MODELING , RENDERING ,
ANIMATION*

INTELLIDRAW
ALDUS CORPORATION
DRAWING

IRAS PC
INTERGRAPH / BENTLEY
SYSTEMS
CADD ON-LINE EDITING

LANTASTIC
ARTISOFT
NETWORK

LAPTRACK
TIMESLIPS CORPORATION
*TIME & EXPENSE TRACKING
FOR LAPTOP*

MAC DRAW PRO
CLARIS
DRAWING 2D

MAC PROJECT PRO
CLARIS CORPORATION
PROJECT MANAGEMENT

MAC WRITE
CLARIS CORPORATION
WORD PROCESSING

MACDRAW PRO
CLARIS CORPORATION
ILLUSTRATION

MACROMEDIA ACTION
MACROMEDIA
2D ANIMATION

MACROMIND 3D
MACROMEDIA
RENDERING & ANIMATION

MACROMIND DIRECTOR
MACROMEDIA
ANIMATION / AUTHORING

MACROMODEL
MACROMEDIA
MODELING

MACWRITE
CLARIS
WORD PROCESSOR

MICRO ARCHITECT
CAD SUPPORT

MICROSOFT MAIL
MICROSOFT
E-MAIL

MICROSOFT OFFICE
MICROSOFT CORPORATION
OFFICE SOLUTIONS

MICROSOFT PROJECT
MICROSOFT CORPORATION
PROJECT MANAGEMENT

MICROSTATION PC
INTERGRAPH / BENTLEY
SYSTEMS
2D / 3D CAD

MICROSTATION REVIEW
INTERGRAPH
CADD ON-LINE REVIEW

MODEL SHOP
MACROMEDIA
CONCEPTUAL MODELING

MODELVIEW
INTERGRAPH
RENDERING & ANIMATION

MYOB
TELEWARE
ACCOUNTING

PAGEMAKER
ALDUS CORPORATION
PAGE LAYOUT DESIGN

PAINTER
FRACTAL DESIGN
CORPORATION
PAINTING

PARADOX
BORLAND
DATABASE

PERSUASION
ALDUS CORPORATION
PRESENTATION

PHOTOSHOP
ADOBE
IMAGE EDITING

PIXAR 128
PIXAR
GRAPHIC TEXTURES

PIXAR TYPESTRY
PIXAR
TYPE DESIGN

POWERPOINT
MICROSOFT
SLIDE PRESENTATION

PREPRINT
ALDUS CORPORATION
PRESENTER PROFESSIONAL

PROJECT
MICROSOFT
PROJECT MANAGEMENT

QUATRO PRO
BORLAND
SPREADSHEET

RENDERMAN GLIMPSE &
SHOWPLACE
PIXAR
RENDERING

RENDERSTAR 2 EXT24
MODERN MEDIUM
RENDERING /ANIMATION

SCHEDULE+
MICROSOFT
*PERSONAL INFORMATION
MANAGER*

SHOWPLACE
PIXAR
SCENE COMPOSITION

SOFT PC
INSIGNIA
FILE CONVERSION

STRATA TYPE 3D
STRATA INC
3D TYPE

STRATA VISION 3D
STRATA INCORPORATED
RENDERING

STUDIOPRO
STRATA VISION INC.
MODELING, RENDERING,
ANIMATION

STUFFIT DELUXE
ALADDIN SYSTEMS INC.
FILE COMPRESSION

SWIVEL 3D PROFESSIONAL
MACROMEDIA
3D MODELING & PRODUCT
DESIGN

TEMPRA MEDIA AUTHOR
MATHEMATICA INC
MULTIMEDIA AUTHORING

TIMESHEET PROFESSIONAL &
TIMESLIPS
TIMESLIPS CORPORATION
TIME AND EXPENSE TRACKING

TS GOLD
TIMBERLINE SOFTWARE
AEC ACCOUNTING

TOPAS PROFESSIONAL
CRYSTAL GRAPHICS
MODELING, RENDERING,
ANIMATION

VG SHADERS VOLS 1, 2 & 3
THE VALIS GROUP
RENDERING

VIRTUS WALKTHROUGH
VIRTUS CORPORATION
ANIMATION

VISUAL DESIGN
SCHREIBER INSTRUMENTS
PLUG-INS FOR ANIMATION

VISUAL INFORMATION
DEVELOPMENT INC (VIDI)
MODELING, RENDERING,
ANIMATION

WORD
MICROSOFT
WORD PROCESSING

MAGAZINE RESOURCES

AIA ONLINE
1735 New York Avenue, NW
Washington, DC 20006
Bulletin board / information service
that caters specifically to the
architectural community.

ALDUS MAGAZINE
Aldus Corporation,
411 First Avenue S. Seattle,
WA 98104-2871
Bimonthly publication. Devoted to
providing users with tips and general
information on Aldus products such
as PageMaker, Freehand, Gallery
Effects, Persuasion, and Fetch.

AMERICA ONLINE
1-800-827-6364
Bulletin board / information service.
It has a very active architecture
forum.

APPLE ENGINEERING / SCIENTIFIC SOLUTIONS GUIDE
20525 Mariani Ave.,
Cupertino, CA 95014
A resource guide. Gives location of
developers who write Macintosh
applications for architecture/
engineering / construction. Also
gives a brief description of the
application.

AUTOCAD 2D
K Street Systems
1600 Stout Street, Suite 300
Denver, CO 80202
Training video tapes that teach you
how to use AutoCAD - 2D.

AUTODESK ANIMATOR PRO VIDEO TRAINING SERIES.
K Street Systems
1600 Stout Street, Suite 300
Denver, CO 80202
Training video tape that teaches you
how to use Animator Pro.

BYTE

Byte Subscription Dept.,
P.O. Box 555
Hightstown, NJ 08520
Very informative magazine, deals with MAC, PC, and Unix platforms. Unbiased, technical coverage of the computer industry.

CD-ROM TODAY

23-00 Route 208
Fair Lawn, NJ 07410
Bi-monthly. Gives the latest information on CD-ROM technology and multimedia.

COMMUNICATING WITH MICROSOFT MAIL

QuickStart
5862 Bolsa Ave., Suite 103
Huntington Beach, CA 92649-1169
A training video.

COMMUNICATION ARTS

410 Sherman Ave., P.O. Box 10300
Palo Alto, CA 94303
Published 8 times a year. Focuses on environmental graphics; not necessarily directly related to computers.

COMPUSERVE

1-800-438-3690
The ultimate information service.

COMPUTER SHOPPER

1 Park Avenue, 11th Floor
New York, NY 10016
Monthly. Packed with information on the computer market. Extensive info for users who buy direct.

DESKTOP VIDEO WORLD

80 Elm St.,
Peterborough, NH 03458
A bimonthly magazine. Video and multimedia products for the Mac, PC, and Amiga machines are presented in this magazine. Extensive review section.

HOME OFFICE COMPUTING
P.O. Box 2511
Boulder, CO 80302
Monthly magazine. Content very true to its title. Addresses issues that affect small business. Everything from software reviews to communications, finance, and business opportunities, all with a small business slant. Very informative.

IN THE STUDIO - WORKING WITH 3D STUDIO Digimation
315 St. Anthony Street,
Luling, LA 70070
A series of five VCR tutorial tapes. It allows you to learn 3D Studio, in your studio, at your own pace. The tapes are broken down into several sections – 2D Shaper, 3D Lofter, 3D Editor, Keyframer, Materials Editor.

INC.
INC Magazine,
P.O. Box 54129
Boulder CO 80322-4129
Monthly magazine.The subheading bills it as "the magazine for growing companies," and that's just what it is. It offers extensive information on marketing and financial strategies. Also does very informative profiles on real businesses. Very helpful information.

INTERACTIVE TRAINING FOR MACROMIND DIRECTOR.
Media in Motion
P.O. Box 170130
San Francisco, CA 94117
A series of interactive disk training.

MACUSER
P.O. Box 56986
Boulder, CO 80321
Monthly. News and information on the Macintosh industry. Interesting feature articles and insightful reviews.

MACWORLD
501 Second Street,
San Francisco, CA 94107
Everything you'll ever want to know about Apple's Macintosh machines. Extensive software and hardware reviews.

MANAGING RESOURCES & COSTS WITH MICROSOFT PROJECT
QuickStart
5862 Bolsa Ave., Suite 103, Huntington Beach, CA 92649-1169
A training video.

MICROSTATION
1580 Center Drive
Santa Fe, NM 87505-9746
Concentrates on Intergraph's MicroStation and other Intergraph products. Addresses other issues affecting architecture and engineering.

MICROSTATION PC - Working in 3D.
K Street Systems
1600 Stout Street, Suite 300
Denver, CO 80202
Training video tape that teaches you how to use MicroStation on the PC or compatible.

MICROSTATION SOLUTIONS
Intergraph Sales Office
Huntsville, Alabama 35894-0001
A listing of third party developers and products that work in conjunction with Intergraph's MicroStation.

NEW MEDIA
New Magazine
P.O. Box 1771
Riverton, NJ 08077-7371
A full-color monthly magazine, showcasing multimedia hardware and software applications. Touches on a wide range of topics, from interactive applications on CD-ROM to software reviews, Q & A and virtual reality.

PC COMPUTING

PC Computing,
P.O.Box 58229
Boulder, CO 80322-8229
Everything you always wanted to know about IBM or compatibles. Extensive product reviews. If you need to know something about a PC product, you'll probably find it here.

PC MAGAZINE

1 Park Avenue
New York, NY 10016
Published biweekly. Does extensive software and hardware reviews for IBM PC and compatibles and their peripherals.

PC SOURCES

P.O. Box 53298 Boulder,
CO 80322-3298
Monthly. Devoted to IBM and compatibles market.

PLANNING

1313 E 60th Street
Chicago, IL 60637
Monthly. Published by the American Planning Association, deals with various issues ranging from urban planning to the use of computers in the built environment.

PRINT

3200 Tower Oaks Blvd.,
Rockville, MD 20852
Bimonthly. A design magazine that is increasingly focusing on how computers can be used in the design process.

PUBLISH

Publish Subscriptions
P.O. Box 55415
Boulder, CO 80322
The magazine for electronic design. Reviews, document makeovers, and how-to articles. Full of information about the process of electronic design.

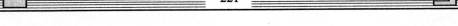

THE AUTOCAD RESOURCE GUIDE

Autodesk Inc.

2320 Marinship Way

Sausalito, CA 94965

A reference for AutoCAD software and related products.

WINDOWS MAGAZINE

600 Community Drive,

Manhasset, NY 11030

Monthly plus two bonus issues. For Windows users – tips, Q & A.

WINDOWS USER

P.O. Box 56628

Boulder, CO 80322-6628

Published monthly. Concentrates on the Windows GUI (graphical user interface).

C4 STUDIO©, Modeled with Form•Z, rendered with StudioPro

INDEX

About the Authors

Karen M. Brown is CEO of C4 Studio – a firm that consults with architecture and design firms about how to make their practice more productive through the use of computer software and hardware technology. C4 Studio, based in Miami, Florida, also specializes in creating three dimensional visual architectural presentations. Ms. Brown is a graduate of Howard University, Washington D.C., where she received her Bachelor of Science.

Curtis B. Charles is a lecturer at the University of Miami, school of architecture – Coral Gables, Florida. He received his bachelor degree in Architecture from Howard University and a Masters of Science in Architectural Studies from Massachusetts Institute of Technology. Mr. Charles is also Project Manager and Lead Designer for C4 Studio.

Both Karen M. Brown and Curtis B. Charles have published articles in Progressive Architecture, American Planning Association Journal, Architecture Records, MicroStation Manager, and other publications.